PIONEERS OF

HIGH, WATER AND MAIN

Reflections of Jefferson City

BY

DR. R. E. YOUNG

FIRST EDITION

TWELFTH STATE JEFFERSON CITY, MISSOURI

Copyright 1997

Twelfth State
P. O. Box 105828
Jefferson City, MO 65110-5828

Printed and bound in the United States of America, September 1997
2   3   4   5   6   7   8   9   10

Library of Congress Cataloging in Publication Data
Young, Dr. Robert E., 1840-1904
        Pioneers of High, Water and Main.
        First Edition.
        Includes Index.
        1. Jefferson City (Mo.) - Social life and customs - General
            Audience.
        2. Missouri - History - Civil War, 1861-1865. I. Title
        Library of Congress Catalog Card Number: 97-61169
        ISBN 0-9659631-7-9

Dedicated...
to past, present, and future members of the Young Family.

Jimmy Dean Murphy

August 17, 1932 - August 20, 1997

ACKNOWLEDGMENTS

Since I began this project, I have had many words of advice and encouragement. There have been many individuals who have helped along the way. I would be unable to name each and list their role individually, but I would like to mention a few of those individuals. I first must mention James E. McGhee, Esq. He was the first to suggest the idea of this publication. Jim provided many suggestions of the layout and as co-author of *Sterling Price's Lieutenants*, he was often consulted about the Missouri State Guard, Lesueur's Battery, and the War Between the States. Mark Schreiber often furnished the much needed encouragement, offered ideas about illustrations, and offered illustrations from his collections. His enthusiasm about this project and past experiences with publishing Jefferson City's history was a tremendous help. Darrell Maples as a "third hand" obtained several of the first names of Dr. Young's comrades in the Missouri State Guard and the Clark Township Southern Guards.

I would also like to extend my gratitude to those who have helped with the research about Dr. Young and his family. The family stories of Billy Murphy, Jimmy Dean Murphy, and Jimmie Eckenberger, all great-great nephews of Dr. Young, have contributed to this book in more ways than they probably know. I thank Billy and Jimmie, the "keepers" of the Young-Murphy archives, for access to family documents and photographs.

The friendly and helpful staff of the Missouri State Archives also merit mentioning. They have always been courteous and congenial with my requests. Laura Jolley, *Archivist*, deserves special mention.

Last but certainly not least, I am indebted to my immediate family. Their support throughout the years, not only with this project but with life in general, has always been of the most-loving character. Mom, Dad, Carleen, and Bob - **Thank you**.

CONTENTS

~

FOREWORD   I

PREFACE   III

THE YOUNG FAMILY   1

THE REMINISCENCES OF DR. R. E. YOUNG   21

WILSON'S CREEK   23
THE GREAT BATTLE FOUGHT 39 YEARS AGO TODAY

JOHN S. MARMADUKE   26

FROM 1848 TO 1851   33
SOMETHING INTERESTING OF JEFFERSON CITY AT THIS TIME

GEN. G. A. PARSONS   36

THE LONG AGO   39
THE OLD THESPIAN SOCIETY OF JEFFERSON CITY

LEGAL TILTS   41
SOME INCIDENTS OF THE PRACTICE OF LAW

JOHN SMITH R.   45
RECOLLECTIONS OF THIS FAMOUS BELLIGERENT

REMINISCENCES   48
DR. YOUNG CONTRIBUTES ANOTHER CHAPTER

THE LONG AGO   51
INTERESTING FACTS CONCERNING THE JEFFERSON CITY
THAT FLOURISHED IN THE EARLY FIFTIES

REMINISCENCES   54
GEN. JAMES L. MINOR'S REPLEVIN SUIT

STORIES   58
OF PEOPLE AND EVENTS IN JEFFERSON CITY

1845-1848   62
ANOTHER INTERESTING LETTER FROM DR. YOUNG

HOW THE BOYS OF JEFFERSON CITY   66
AMUSED THEMSELVES YEARS AGO

RETROSPECTIVE   70
DR. YOUNG'S REMINISCENCES OF THE DAYS LONG AGO.
INTERESTING ANECDOTES AND SKETCHES OF
JEFFERSON CITY'S CITIZENS OF ANTEBELLUM DAYS

HOW PEOPLE USED TO GO TO CHURCH   74
IN JEFFERSON CITY

CHANGES THAT HAVE OCCURRED   78
IN JEFFERSON CITY

A BIT OF HISTORY   82
CONCERNING A CONTRACT BETWEEN
THE STATE AND JEFFERSON CITY

**POLITICS AT THE STATE
CAPITAL FIFTY YEARS AGO**   86

GHOST STORY   92
HOW BURR MCCARTY GOT BLACK HAWK TO SHOW SPEED

A CHARIVARI   96
HOW GEN. BOLTON AND WIFE TRIED TO ESCAPE ONE

FOOLED HIS WIFE   100
HOW DR. POPE DORRIS ATTENDED A BALL

OLDEN TIMES   104
A STORY TOLD ON DR. TENNESSEE MATHEWS

AN XMAS SCRAP   107
THAT OCCURRED MORE THAN FIFTY YEARS AGO

HENRY PAULSEL   110
A HIGHLY POLISHED GENTLEMAN STOOD BY A FRIEND

THE BATTLE OF HELENA   113

OLD-TIMERS   119
PERPETUAL MOTION MADE A POOR MAN OF JNO. BAUER

DOCTOR BERRY   123
A BELL OVER THE DOOR ANNOUNCED HIS CUSTOMERS

W. E. DUNSCOMB   127
HELD THREE IMPORTANT POSITIONS AT THE CAPITOL

OLD TANYARD   131
HOW LEATHER WAS TANNED YEARS AGO IN THIS CITY

JUDGE EDWARDS   136
WAS THE FRIEND OF THE YOUNG MAN

BOYS' TROUBLES   140
"DON'T CRY, BUT STRIKE BACK," SAID THE FATHER

REMINISCENCES OF OLD-TIMERS   145

WEDDINGS IN JEFFERSON CITY   149
IN OLDEN TIMES

HOBO HILL   154
THE OLD SCHOOL HOUSE OF OUR FATHERS

THE COUNTRY   158
PEOPLE WHO LIVED AROUND JEFFERSON CITY

OTHER ARTICLES CONCERNING DR. YOUNG   163

APPENDIX A   187
MAP OF 1849 JEFFERSON CITY

APPENDIX B   190
SOLDIERS OF THE MEXICAN WAR

APPENDIX C   191
SOLDIERS OF THE WAR BETWEEN THE STATES

APPENDIX D   192
CLARK TOWNSHIP SOUTHERN GUARDS

BIBLIOGRAPHY   193

SOURCES OF ILLUSTRATIONS   199

INDEX   201

ILLUSTRATIONS

~

VIEW OF 1859 JEFFERSON CITY
AND THE YOUNG FAMILY TREE   2

WILLIAM CAMPBELL YOUNG   5

THE YOUNG FAMILY MONUMENTS   14

DR. ROBERT EMMET YOUNG   15

THE YOUNG RESIDENCE ON MAIN STREET   16

THE YOUNG RESIDENCE TODAY   17

WILLIAM CAMPBELL YOUNG, II   18

JAMES MCKENNA YOUNG   19

DR. YOUNG IN HIS OFFICE   20

GENERAL LYON'S CHARGE AT WILSON'S CREEK   22

JOHN SAPPINGTON MARMADUKE   27

MOSBY MONROE PARSONS   37

THE OLD COURTHOUSE   43

JEFFERSON INQUIRER PRINTING OFFICE   61

THE OLD EXECUTIVE OFFICE AND MANSION   65

THE STATE CAPITOL OF 1840   85

THE FERGUSON HOUSE   87

THOMAS LAWSON PRICE   89

PRICE MANSION   91

BURR HARRISON MCCARTY   93

WILLIAM H. LUSK   97

NEWMAN'S CITY HOTEL   109

CONFEDERATE SOLDIERS   113

EDWARD LIVINGSTON EDWARDS   134

THOMAS MILLER WINSTON   144

PHILLIP THOMAS MILLER   151

CLONEY, CRAWFORD & CO.   153

SIGNATURE OF R. E YOUNG   162

PRIVATE ROBERT "BOB" E. YOUNG   178

FOREWORD

Each year there appear in bookstores and on newsstands new publications in an almost endless variety addressing a broad spectrum of historic events and subjects. All too often authors examine an event or subject as the big picture and fail to address issues in detail, the seemingly insignificant daily events which capture a reader's interest. Such is not the case in *Pioneers of High, Water, and Main*, a collection of reminiscences reflected by Dr. R. E. Young, a colorful pioneer physician of Jefferson City, Missouri.

Unaware at the time what he would be contributing to future generations of readers, Dr. Young wrote a series of historical and biographical sketches that appeared in the columns of a local Jefferson City newspaper between the years 1900-1901. Through the often graphic descriptions given by Dr. Young, the student of Jefferson City and Missouri history will be captivated by both the events and the pioneer spirit of the men and women who came to the edge of the western frontier and made things happen.

Many of those who came were direct descendants of patriot colonists from Virginia and the Carolinas who fought in the American Revolution. Several, including Christopher Casey and John Gordon, were themselves patriot soldiers. Through the efforts of early pioneers, the City of Jefferson was born and became the permanent capital of Missouri.

From childhood friendships, epidemics, murders, weddings, hangings, and religious events to the tragically difficult years of the War Between the States, descriptions of events and the characters who made them are brought to life by Dr. Young.

Almost one hundred years from the date of Dr. Young's publications, a twenty-two year-old historian was conducting research, unaware that his life and that of his ancestor, Dr. Young, were about to cross paths. Ed Ziehmer, a great nephew of Dr. R. E. Young, shares a mutual interest in events and people and thus a partnership was formed bridging one generation with another.

Taking the words drafted by his ancestor, Ziehmer has compiled them into a unique volume presented here. Through a skillful combination of research, graphics, photographs, and maps, Ziehmer has unselfishly regenerated his ancestor's literary gift so others may enjoy life as it was in 19th century Jefferson City. East Main Street (East Capitol Avenue), Water Street (State Street), McCarty Street, High Street, the Missouri State Penitentiary (JCCC), the home of John C. Gordon (Buescher Funeral Home) and the Bolton residence on Green Berry Road, all still evident today, are part of our 19th century heritage. Many of the names recorded by the pen of Dr. Young can now be found etched on the tombstones of eternity at the Woodland and Old City Cemeteries.

Ed Ziehmer, like R. E. Young, has a realization that each of us is a unique part of history no matter how seemingly insignificant. Only by sharing with others where we have been can those who follow us have a sense of where they are going; for after all, a life without memory in any generation is no life at all.

Mark S. Schreiber
President
1996-1997-1998
Missouri Society,
Sons of the American Revolution

PREFACE

In quest of my ancestral roots, I came across a series of letters written by Dr. R. E. Young in a local newspaper during the period 1900-1901. These letters immediately received my attention as they were written by my great-great-great grandmother's only brother. After sharing a few of these reminiscences with family and friends, I was encouraged to print them in booklet format. As can be seen, I took the suggestions a few steps further.

In compiling these letters, I experienced a wide range of emotions. I was excited to read fascinating, social accounts of Missouri's capital city but unfortunately, my sources were limited to the microfilm reels at the State Historical Society in Columbia. Some issues of the paper were damaged or illegible due to the quality of filming. The original papers were destroyed before the quality of the film was checked.

Sometimes, in place of illegible text, it became necessary to substitute a neutral word or two. Though the substituted words are few, the reader should be aware of what was done. Historical accuracy has been the highest priority. The letters are as Dr. Young wrote them.

In some cases, issues containing Dr. Young's letters were missing and not available for filming. There are about half a dozen articles believed to have been written by Dr. Young which I have been unable to locate through various resources. As you read through this volume, it will become evident where the missing letters belong. My search for these issues will continue.

Throughout the letters, names such as Basye and Dunnica were misprinted as Basey and Dunica. When possible, names printed within the letters were verified and accurate spellings provided. It was common for the "county" in "Cole County" and other such words capitalized today not to be capitalized or vice versa. Occasionally, there may be inconsistencies in capitalization. The intent was to copy these words exactly as they appeared. Due to the often fuzzy images of the microfilm, punctuation was hard to recognize and used at the editor's discretion to aid the modern-day reader in comprehending the sometimes complex and lengthy sentences used long ago.

Remember the letters were written nearly a century ago. The structure and use of the language may be awkward and sometimes offending. But if you remember the times, I am sure you will find the letters fascinating. If you enjoy reading this book half as much as I enjoyed publishing it, you will not be disappointed.

There have been two major driving forces that have motivated me to spend the time and money planning and coordinating this project. First, was to make readily available a first-hand account of our local heritage. Researchers can spend a lifetime discovering facts and figures but mere statistics lack the rich detail that accurately describes the people and society of yesteryear.

The importance of the letters will become evident as the pages turn. Dr. Young offers a first-hand view of Jefferson City and its social characteristics one hundred and fifty years ago. True, many of the facts contained in Dr. Young's letters may be found in the State Archives or the State Historical Society but many of the physical and behavioral descriptions of those he knew are only found within his personal recollections.

Secondly, along with providing a true, accurate account of Jefferson City's heritage, I have the hope this book will inspire the readers to write of their own experiences. In understanding the importance of studying our heritage, we can appreciate the fact that we must ensure future generations have access to historically accurate accounts of our society so they may make decisions based upon knowledge of our failures and accomplishments. As a genealogist, there is no greater find than the personal recollections of a grandfather, grandmother, or another family member. Words of long ago offer more than any census or public record ever can.

Ed Ziehmer

THE

YOUNG FAMILY

OF

JEFFERSON CITY

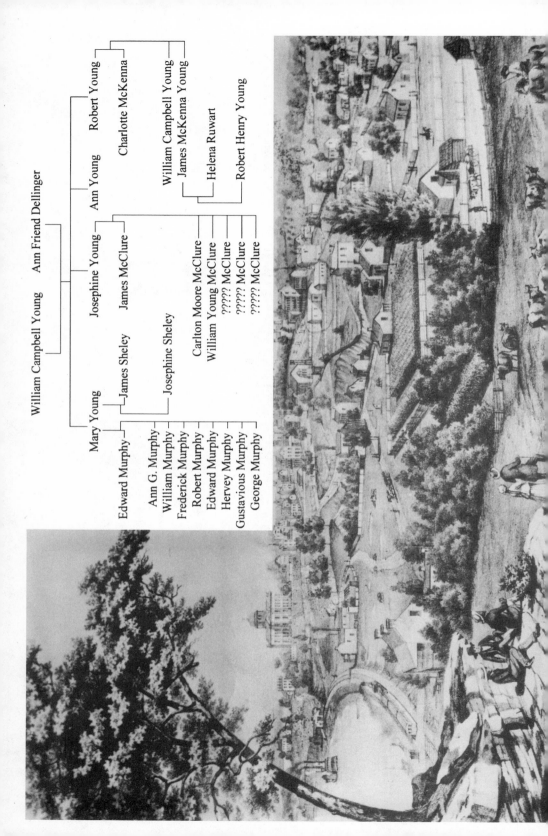

William Campbell Young — Ann Friend Dellinger

Mary Young — James Sheley

Josephine Young — James McClure

Ann Young — Robert Young

Charlotte McKenna

Josephine Sheley

Edward Murphy

Ann G. Murphy
William Murphy
Frederick Murphy
Robert Murphy
Edward Murphy
Hervey Murphy
Gustavious Murphy
George Murphy

Carlton Moore McClure
William Young McClure
????? McClure
????? McClure
????? McClure

William Campbell Young
James McKenna Young — Helena Ruwart

Robert Henry Young

The story of Robert Emmet Young extends beyond his own defeats and accomplishments. He was constantly influenced by the members of his family and the citizens of Jefferson City. Those who followed him, were in turn left with lasting impressions of one of Cole County's most colorful characters. Dr. Young was, as is everyone, a bridge supported by the foundation of his forefathers' societies and spanning into the society of which he was a direct influence.

William Campbell Young, Robert's father, was a strong influence upon his son's personality. William Campbell Young was born on August 12, 1813 in County Down, Ireland.[1] At the age of seven, William C. Young immigrated to America with his father, Moses. No doubt, Moses had great expectations of America and the opportunities the New World would afford his family. The opportunities eventually led William to the "Land of the Big Canoe." Becoming active in politics and other community affairs, William C. Young became an influential citizen in the early days of Missouri's capital city. But before his journeys brought him to Jefferson City, he grew to manhood in the east.[2]

While a young man, he became apprenticed to the carpenter's trade and learned the skills that helped to secure him a place in our local history. William C. Young was one of the contractors on the State Capitol building (1838-40) and later superintendent of construction.[3] After the capitol was completed, he continued to contract and build other important public buildings. The courthouses of Camden (1846),[4] Morgan (1844),[5] and Wright (1849)[6] counties as well as the foundation of the 1847 courthouse in Moniteau County[7] were constructed with his talents. His proven skills were also in demand by private citizens. The extravagant residence of General Thomas Lawson Price was one of his accomplishments.[8]

William C. Young did not limit himself to contracting but was actively engaged in many other activities. In 1838, he was appointed judge advocate of the Missouri State Militia and held the rank of colonel.[9] It is uncertain how long he officially held this position but he was known as Colonel Young until the War Between the States. Colonel Young could be found operating the City Hotel for a short period in 1840-41 without success.[10] Nearly broke from this business venture, he went back to contracting for a living.

Although he could not attract the necessary guests to successfully operate the hotel, he became active in politics and received his share of the votes cast in Cole County during the mid-1800s. In 1856, he was elected justice of the Cole County court for two years.[11] As a steadfast anti-Benton Democrat, he was not only popular with the voters of Cole County but with other elected officials of the county and state as well. Shortly after his election to the county bench, he accepted the appointment as Factor of the Missouri State Penitentiary by Governor Sterling Price in August of 1856.[12] He resigned as judge and on August 26, officially filled the office of factor.[13] Upon the death of Judge Robert A. Ewing, he was again commissioned as a justice of the Cole County court on December 30, 1857.[14] Ewing had been elected in 1856 for a term of six years and in August 1858, Young was elected by the people to complete the remaining four years of Ewing's term.[15] But after the test oath ordinance passed in 1862, S. H. Legg was commissioned in place of the secessionist Judge W. C. Young.[16] After the war and his enfranchisement, he was again elected justice of the Cole County court in 1874.[17]

Judge Young was not only a popular politician but also an active member of the business and social community. He was elected to the board of directors of the First National Bank of Jefferson City and in January 1889, became president of the bank, a position he held until 1891.[18] On April 7, 1847, he was initiated into the Jefferson Lodge No. 43, A. F. & A. M.[19]

But before William C. Young became Colonel Young and Judge Young and while still living in the east, he became acquainted with Miss Ann "Nancy" Friend Dellinger, daughter of Henry and Catherine Dellinger of Washington County, Maryland.[20] In late 1833, they desired to be married but were unable to unite in marriage under the laws of Maryland as they were not of the legal age. On December 24, 1833 they eloped across the state line into Virginia near Williamsport and exchanged their vows on Christmas Day.[21]

When William C. and Ann F. Young emigrated to Jefferson City in 1837, the Dellinger family also came west. Ann F. Young became a popular social and Christian figure in and around Jefferson City. The silver communion service at the Cumberland Presbyterian Church of Centertown was presented by her.[22] Ann Young died on December 28, 1889 in her 75th year and William Young died on September 19, 1895.[23]

WILLIAM CAMPBELL YOUNG

William C. and Ann F. Young raised a family of children and grandchildren who were also popular and influential. They had three daughters, Mary Catherine, Josephine, and Ann J. and one son, Robert Emmet.

The oldest child of William and Ann Young was Mary Catherine. She was born in Maryland on November 9, 1834.[24] Mary would first marry Edward Gustavious Murphy of Linn Creek, Missouri, a man of notable importance and pedigree in Missouri.[25] Edward G. Murphy was born on April 20, 1832[26] and descended from an old and influential Missouri family. His father, William Dubart Murphy, was a partner of McClurg, Murphy & Co. and operated a steamboat shipping business in Linn Creek.[27] Joseph W. McClurg, the soon to be Governor and Congressman, was Edward G. Murphy's brother-in-law.[28] Edward G. Murphy's great-grandfather, Rev. William Murphy, had made land claims with the Spanish government in March 1798.[29] This area became known as Murphy's Settlement and was later incorporated as Farmington, Missouri.[30] His great-grandmother was Sarah Barton Murphy, aunt of David Barton, Missouri's first United States Senator and author of Missouri's first constitution.[31] Sarah Barton Murphy is credited with starting the first Protestant Sunday School west of the Mississippi River.[32]

Edward G. Murphy and Mary Catherine Young were married in Jefferson City on October 4, 1855.[33] They had eight children, one daughter and seven sons.

Ann G. Murphy, Edward and Mary Murphy's oldest child, was born on October 4, 1856 and died on May 12, 1857.[34] Ann Murphy is buried in Woodland Cemetery in Jefferson City.

William Emmet, the oldest son of Edward and Mary Murphy, was born on December 24, 1857.[35] On June 20, 1894, he was married to Lillie Ann Anderson, daughter of William and Minerva Ann Fletcher Anderson.[36] To this marriage were born two sons, Edward Anderson and Robert Gustavious. William Emmet was elected judge of the second district of Cole County in 1900 and re-elected in 1902.[37] He died on June 3, 1903 and is buried in the Centertown Cemetery, Cole County.[38]

Frederick Young Murphy, the third child of Edward and Mary Murphy, was born November 19, 1859.[39] Together with his brother William, he operated his Grandfather William C. Young's farm under the name of F. Y. Murphy & Bro., thus the farm became known as Murphy's Ford near Lohman, Cole County, Missouri.[40] Frederick Murphy married Ollie Yows on March 18th, 1896. They had five children, Kenneth, Florence, Mary Catherine, Helen, and F. Y. Jr.[41] Frederick Murphy died on February 25, 1941[42] and is buried in the Centertown Cemetery, Cole County.

Robert Lee Murphy, the fourth child of Edward and Mary Murphy, was born August 29, 1862.[43] He succumbed to the dreaded typhoid fever and died at the residence of his Grandfather Young on August 9, 1883. He was at the time employed at the Bank of Commerce in St. Louis.[44]

Edward Shay Murphy, the fifth child of Edward and Mary Murphy, was born on April 12, 1864 and lived but a few months, dying on July 3, 1864.[45]

Hervey Ayres Murphy, the sixth child of Edward and Mary Murphy, was born May 12, 1865.[46] He never married and died on April 15, 1934.[47] He is buried near his eldest two brothers in the Centertown Cemetery.

Gustavious McClure Murphy, the seventh child of Edward and Mary Murphy, was born November 11, 1867.[48] Like his brothers Robert and Hervey, he never married. Gus died on July 23, 1899 at the home of his brother William near Centertown, Missouri.[49] He had been employed in several county offices in Jackson County, Missouri and just prior to his death, accepted a position in the Jackson County Assessor's office.[50]

George E. Murphy, the eighth child of Edward and Mary Murphy, was born on August 17, 1869 and died August 29, 1871.[51]

Pneumonia took the life of Edward G. Murphy on April 20, 1869, his 37th birthday.[52] Edward G. Murphy is buried in a now unmarked grave in the Old City Cemetery in Jefferson City.[53]

After Edward G. Murphy's death, Mary married James K. Sheley on August 5, 1873 and moved to Independence, Missouri.[54] On March 4, 1893, Mary Catherine Young Murphy Sheley died and James K. Sheley died on November 6, 1893.[55] They had one daughter, Josephine Sheley, who was born February 17, 1875.[56] Josephine married William C. Hall, had a son, Charles Edward Hall, and died in Boston on June 2, 1928.[57]

Jospehine C. was the second child of William C. and Ann F. Young. On October 21, 1858, she married James R. McClure of Philadelphia.[58] Two of their children died in infancy and are buried in Woodland Cemetery in Jefferson City. Carlton Moore McClure died November 2, 1860 at the age of 15 months and William Young McClure died February 5, 1861 at the age of three and a half months.[59] There were three other children.[60]

Ann J., the third child of William and Ann Young, died at the age of 16 on August 1, 1855.[61] Her memory has been etched into history on the same monument as her niece, Ann G. Murphy.

The youngest child of William and Ann Young was Robert Emmet, named for his father's fondness of the Irish Patriot.[62] Robert Emmet was born in Jefferson City on February 29, 1840[63] in a house on the corner of Jefferson and Main (East Capitol).[64] After being educated in the schools in and around Jefferson City, he attended the University of Missouri at Columbia. Robert Young continued his education at the State University until May 1861 when he could no longer avoid the perils of the political atmosphere and the resulting war that had began many years before as the Border Wars.[65]

In Jefferson City, largely due to the election of Lincoln, the "political excitement rose to a very high pitch"[66] during the winter of 1860-61. It became common for the citizens to be "cussing and discussing things in general and Old Abe, in particular."[67] Late in the evening of May 9, 1861, Governor Claiborne Jackson received warning that the Federals intended to attack the capital city.[68] "The church bells were rung, the people flocked to the capitol, [and] the representatives were in their seats, muskets in hand."[69] The next day the Federals captured Camp Jackson near St. Louis. As the prisoners were being marched to the St. Louis arsenal, the crowd became unruly. Shots were fired by the Federals killing 28 persons including a woman holding a baby.[70]

Upon hearing the reports of Camp Jackson and the possibility of such an event occurring in Jefferson City, Robert left the university in his junior year and returned to his native town where during the day "on May 9 there [had been] a grand secession flag-raising, the Legislature adjourning to attend."[71] On May 10, the state legislature met in special session and made provisions for the Missouri State Guard. When Robert Young arrived in Jefferson City on May 12, he enlisted in Company B of

Col. Robert A. McCulloch's 1st Cavalry Regiment, Sixth Division, Missouri State Guard for a term of six months. This local company, known as the Clark Township Southern Guards, was commanded by Fountain McKenzie and had been organized on February 6, 1861.[72]

He was one of the thousands of men who "poured in all day...in compliance with the call of the Governor... ready to be sent into the thickest of the fight" when "the news that the Capital [was] threatened with an attack...spread like wildfire through the country."[73] The arrival of these troops was "enthusiastically cheered by crowds of citizens as well as the soldiers already arrived."[74] The condition in the capital city was emotional as it was reported that "but one cry has been heard in the streets of Jefferson City, and that is 'hurrah for the Governor!' Those who have been known to stand firmest to the Union are silenced, while among those who were wavering the Union sentiments [have] been completely crushed out by the recent events in St. Louis."[75]

Robert "Bob" Young was immediately detailed as the orderly of General Mosby Monroe Parsons, an old family friend.[76] When the state government and the Missouri State Guard left the capital city, Bob was with them and would not see his native city again for five years. After the battles of Carthage (July 5, 1861) and Oak Hills (Wilson's Creek), Private Young became a hardened veteran of warfare. At Oak Hills, his young life was spared by the "God of Battles" and General Parsons praised his bravery.[77]

Bob was also with the Missourians at the siege of Lexington (also known as the "Battle of the Hemp Bales"). The secession sentiment throughout the state had became strong and widespread at this time. On October 28, 1861, the elected government of Missouri passed an ordinance of secession. Governor Claiborne Jackson signed the ordinance three days later and on October 31,[78] as far they were concerned, "all political connection between the government of the United States of America, and the people and government of the State of Missouri, [were] dissolved."[79] Missouri, under the elected government of 1860, was subsequently admitted into the Confederate States of America on November 28, 1861.[80]

Also in November, when his original enlistment had ended, Bob re-enlisted in Company I of the same regiment of cavalry.[81] In 1862, after many Missouri State Guardsmen had transferred to the Confederate States Army with the encouragement of Sterling Price, Bob could still be found in the ranks of the Missouri State Guard fighting for Southern Independence with General Parsons. He saw action at Elkhorn Tavern (Pea Ridge) in March 1862,[82] after which he became very ill. The few military records that exist indicate that he was in the hospital at Memphis,[83] which probably occurred shortly after this battle when the Missouri troops crossed the Mississippi River. In May 1862, he was with Parsons during the siege of Corinth, Mississippi.[84] He then enlisted in the Confederate States Army on the retreat to Tupelo. Afterwards, he was transferred to Guibor's battery for a couple of weeks, after which time he was then transferred to Gorham's battery. Gorham's battery became known as the Third Missouri or Lesueur's battery. [85]

Bob was with Alexander A. Lesueur, a future Missouri Secretary of State, during those fateful days of July 3-4, 1863 when the Confederate forces experienced three major defeats. Gettysburg was lost by the Army of Northern Virginia after two days of fighting. The Federals occupied Vicksburg, Mississippi on July 4 after a lengthy siege of that town. Also on July 4, the Army of the Trans-Mississippi went on the offensive and was defeated at the battle of Helena, Arkansas.

Bob participated in the Red River campaign of 1864 including the battles of Pleasant Hill and Jenkin's Ferry. In the spring of 1865, he was detailed as sergeant-in-charge of the arsenal while camped at Camden, Arkansas.[86] His obituary says he served with a Louisiana company at the end of the war. His parole records indicate, however, that if he had been with any other company, he had rejoined the Third Missouri Battery and surrendered with that unit and was paroled on June 17, 1865.[87]

After his parole, he lived in Louisiana and taught school.[88] He reportedly stayed in Louisiana to raise the necessary money to return to his native home where his family had endured many hardships. Robert may have been loath to return to Missouri for other reasons, especially if he was aware of his father's arrest, removal from the county bench, and temporary sentence to be banished from Missouri. After about 18 months in Louisiana, he did return to his father's farm, where he worked and continued his education at the University of Missouri.[89]

Upon completing his degree at the University of Missouri, he studied medicine and surgery at the University of Pennsylvania where he graduated in 1871.[90] With his medical degree, he returned once more to

Jefferson City where he began a career that would bring him notoriety not only in Cole County but throughout Missouri.

Dr. Robert E. Young immediately became active in the affairs of his profession and became a charter member and recording secretary of the 1873 Medical Society of Central Missouri.[91] In 1873, Dr. Young was appointed physician of the Missouri State Penitentiary by Governor Silas Woodson.[92] Dr. Young held this position for two years. The governor also appointed him to the National Prison Reform Congress in May 1874.[93]

Newspaper accounts report in 1875 that he had moved to St. Louis. He was living back in Jefferson City, however, by Christmas of the same year. It was also reported that when he was crossing the Moreau River in October 1877, he was thrown from his horse.[94] Although subjected to great bodily harm during this incident, he escaped injury. The "God of battles," which had watched over the young soldier during the great war, had once again preserved the doctor.

Dr. Young would experience more difficulties and defeats. Like his father, he became active in local politics. In 1874, he was defeated as a mayoral candidate in Jefferson City as one of three Democrats on the ticket.[95] In 1880, he ran for county coroner and lost the election to John B. Pondrom by a vote of 1,442 to 1,316.[96]

But these defeats did not keep Dr. Young from running for other public offices. In 1877 he was elected Cole County School Commissioner and was re-elected in each election until 1885.[97] In 1880, he received 181 votes for First Ward Alderman against the other two candidates' one vote each.[98] He completed the one-year term and did not seek the office again.

He not only served his community in public office but was also active in social affairs. On June 7, 1882, Dr. Young was one of several members to acknowledge the incorporation of the Cole County Fair Association.[99] And while living in Nevada, Missouri, Dr. Young was also elected president of the Nevada Fair Association.[100]

In the years after the war, Dr. Young became acquainted with the famous Confederate General John Sappington Marmaduke and after the latter became Governor in 1884, they enjoyed an intimate friendship. In January 1885, to fill a vacancy, Governor Marmaduke approved the Senate's appointment of Dr. Young to the Board of Regents of Lincoln

Institute.[101] Dr. Young was again commissioned in January 1887 to this board for a term of six years.[102]

The Marmaduke administration also appointed him in April 1886 to the Board of Commissioners of the State Lunatic Asylum No. 3 located at Nevada, Mo in Vernon County.[103] He resigned from this position after he was chosen to be the superintendent of the asylum in June 1887.[104] In 1889, while living in Nevada, Dr. Young received the grim news of the imminent death of the great governor and returned to Jefferson City to attend to the last wishes of his close friend.

Governor Marmaduke was so beloved by the citizens of Missouri, Cole County, and the family of Dr. Young, that they created and named memorials in his honor. Dr. Young's nephews, Frederick and William E. Murphy, even named their finest English stallion "John S. Marmaduke."[105] Dr. Young himself oversaw the construction of the Marmaduke Park near the Nevada Asylum.[106] He supervised its maintenance until he resigned as superintendent of the asylum in 1893 and returned to his native city.[107]

Once again, Dr. Young established his private practice and continued his interest in community and political affairs in Jefferson City. In January 1895, he was appointed vice-president of the First National Bank of Jefferson City and held that position until his death.[108] He was Cole County Democratic Chairman for many years.[109] In 1897, he was appointed to the State Board of Charities and Corrections[110] and held that position until he resigned on January 31, 1901.[111]

Dr. Young was also a prominent member of several community and professional organizations. He was a Mason and a member of the Jefferson Lodge No. 43 A. F. and A. M.[112] The A. O. U. W. Capital Lodge 67 gave Dr. Young the honor of being its medical examiner.[113] The Prince of Peace Commandery No. 29, Knights Templar and the Benevolent Association also had the good doctor in their membership.[114] When the Central Missouri District Medical Society was organized in 1897, the membership chose Dr. Young as its first president.[115] The Cole County Medical Society also elected Dr. Young as its leader upon its formation in 1903.[116]

He was also active in preserving the memory of his past comrades-at-arms. Dr. Young was a charter member of the General Mosby Monroe Parsons Camp No. 718, United Confederate Veterans. In the Sixth Annual Reunion (1902) book of the Missouri Division, he is listed as one of forty-five members of the Parsons Camp No. 718. Dr. Young attended several reunions of the Confederates.

During the winter of 1872-73, Dr. Young made the acquaintance of Miss Charlotte McKenna. She was born May 22, 1840 in Indiana, Pennsylvania and met Dr. Young while in Jefferson City visiting her sister, Mrs. J. Ed Belch.[117] Dr. Robert Emmet Young and Charlotte McKenna were married in Philadelphia on May 21, 1873.[118] Like her husband, Mrs. Young became an esteemed and popular member of the community. She was active in church, social, and civic activities and had a large circle of friends.

Dr. and Mrs. Young soon made their home on Main Street in the houses now addressed as 514 and 516 E. Capitol.[119] On the bottom step leading up to the entrance of the house at 516 E. Capitol, the words "Dr. Young," though faint and worn, are left as a reminder to the present passerby of the early inhabitants of the house.

Dr. and Mrs. Young became the parents of two sons, William Campbell and James McKenna.[120] William Campbell Young was born on January 17, 1875.[121] He followed his father's footsteps into the medical profession and became a dentist in Jefferson City. In 1900, he practiced his profession with his father in the Dallmeyer Building.[122] Dr. William C. Young never married and died at his mother's residence at 514 East Main Street [East Capitol Ave] on September 27, 1915.[123]

James McKenna Young was born June 25, 1876.[124] He operated the Young Grocery Company at the southeast corner of High and Madison streets.[125] On October 23, 1901 James McKenna married Helena Ruwart, the daughter of Henry Ruwart of Jefferson City.[126] They had one son, Robert Henry who was born July 26, 1902.[127]

Dr. Robert Emmet Young passed from this life on January 8, 1904.[128] He is buried in Woodland Cemetery next to his parents, William C. and Ann Friend Young, his sister Ann, his niece Ann Murphy, his son William, and the wife of General Mosby Monroe Parsons. The Dellinger family, including his maternal grandparents, Henry and Catherine Dellinger, are buried nearby in the Old City Cemetery as well as his brother-in-law, Edward G. Murphy. His good friend, Governor Marmaduke, rests several feet away in the state burial lot. As in life, he is in death surrounded by family and friends.

THE YOUNG FAMILY MONUMENTS IN WOODLAND CEMETERY, JEFFERSON CITY, MISSOURI. THE WHITE STONE ON THE LEFT IS HEADSTONE OF ROBERT EMMET YOUNG, THE TALL GRANITE MONUMENT MARKS THE GRAVES OF HIS FATHER, WILLIAM C. YOUNG, AND HIS MOTHER, ANN F. YOUNG. THE RIGHTMOST HEADSTONE BEARS THE NAMES OF ANN J. YOUNG AND ANN G. MURPHY. THE IRON FENCE IMMEDIATELY BEHIND ROBERT EMMET'S MARKER SURROUNDS THE GRAVES OF MARY PARSONS, THE WIFE OF MOSBY MONROE PARSONS, AND THEIR DAUGHTER, JOSEPHINE PARSONS. THERE IS ALSO A MEMORIAL STONE FOR M. M. PARSONS WHO WAS KILLED IN OLD MEXICO AFTER THE WAR BETWEEN THE STATES.

DR. ROBERT EMMET YOUNG

THE YOUNG FAMILY RESIDENCE AT **514 - 516 EAST CAPITOL** TODAY (ABOVE) AND AS IT LOOKED A CENTURY AGO (OPPOSITE) WHEN THE STREET WAS STILL NAMED **EAST MAIN.**

WILLIAM CAMPBELL YOUNG, II

JAMES MCKENNA YOUNG

THE

REMINISCENCES

OF

DR. R. E. YOUNG

WILSON'S CREEK
THE GREAT BATTLE FOUGHT 39 YEARS AGO TODAY

THE MISSOURI STATE TRIBUNE, FRIDAY EVENING AUGUST 10, 1900
PAGE 1, COLUMNS 1-2

Jefferson City, Aug. 10, 1900

To the Editor of the State Tribune:

Today, thirty-nine years ago was fought the battle of Wilson's Creek. The night before, Gen. M. M. Parsons' brigade of Price's army was camped about Sharp's house - the infantry and artillery north of the house and the cavalry to the south in an open field. Headquarters was just down the hill in the flat north of Sharp's house and [Col. Joseph] Kelly's infantry and [Henry] Guibor's battery were north of headquarters. I belonged to [Fountain] McKenzie's company of [Robert A.] Bob McCulloch's regiment of cavalry but at that time was detailed as Gen. Parsons' orderly and of course was with the staff at headquarters. I had been ordered by the General to keep my horse saddled and bridled for we expected to make a night march toward Springfield. At 9 p.m. the orders came from Gen. [Sterling] Price to camp for the night but Gen. Parsons ordered me to keep my horse saddled until further orders. Not getting any further orders, I laid down on my blanket near him until morning.

At daylight, I called up Parsons' cook Sid, a bright colored boy, the General's servant, and whom he had brought with him from home. Sid soon had breakfast, such as it was, ready - roasting ears, coffee (made of cornmeal browned) and "sow belly." The General and I breakfasted together although I was a private soldier on detail. The General had known me from infancy and always treated me socially as though I was his own son. The General was a small eater and was soon done and ordered his horse, a beautiful blooded bay with black mane and tall black legs, not a white hair on him, to be saddled. He sat there joking me about my eating and declaring that I ate so much it made me poor to carry it. I was about the sparest-built man in camp. Capt. [Austin] Standish,[*] adjutant of staff, being nearly as slim as

---

[*] rank was Colonel and is correct throughout the rest of this letter

myself, often said: "Bob, you and I are safe if we keep sideways to the enemy for we are so thin we would split a bullet."

While we were talking and I still eating, a twig from a sycamore fell down on the camp table and immediately we heard the report of a cannon on our extreme left toward Springfield. General Parsons immediately mounted and ordered me to do likewise and to call his staff which was camped a little further toward Springfield than the General and I. I found them mounted and we were all soon about the General awaiting orders and he awaiting orders from General Price. The orders soon came to form his brigade to the left of the road to Springfield and on a wooded eminence immediately on our left. The General's staff and Guibor's battery led the way but before the infantry could cross the road, an endless stream of fleeing baggage wagons so blocked the road that the infantry which had formed in their camp on the right of the road could not cross.

As soon as General Parsons had found a position for his battery, he turned to Lieut. [James T.] Jim Edwards,* his aide-de-camp, and ordered him to tell Kelly to form on his left and to bring the cavalry and form them on our right. Lieut. Edwards* started to deliver the orders to Col. Kelly when his horse was killed and he was afoot. The General then asked me if I knew where Kelly's regiment was. I answered: "I will find it." He said: "Tell the colonel to move up rapidly and form to the left of the battery."

All this time, Guibor was pouring shot and shell into the advancing foe. I found Colonel Kelly with his regiment drawn up on the road by his camp awaiting orders, or rather waiting for the wagons to clear the road so he could cross. Just as I reached him the road cleared somewhat and I delivered my message. The Colonel said: "Bob, show me where the battery is (everybody in the brigade knew me as Bob, the man that rode the bobtail gray horse)." I succeeded in leading them to where the battery was and as the regiment was wheeling into line and while I was still between the enemy and Kelly's regiment, a volley from the hidden foe swept over us and about us like hailstones. Charley O'Malley, my poor, faithful horse that my father gave me to ride away to the war, fell to rise no more. As he sank beneath me, he neighed and some of my comrades always said I cried. Be that as it may, I never saw his like again.

---

* actually Lieutenant-Colonel Jim Edwards

On foot I reported to the General that the regiment was formed as he had ordered and was paying its compliments to the enemy and that I awaited further orders. He said: "Well done, my boy, get mounted if you can; if not do as you please." I joined Captain [James Rockne "Rock"] Champion who was by this time in command of Kelly's regiment, the colonel having been wounded and Lieutenant-Colonel [Stephen O.] Coleman having been killed.

At the time Edwards and I had been sent after Kelly's regiment, Col. Standish had been sent after McCulloch's cavalry but by this time General [Franz] Sigel had turned our right and cut the cavalry off [and] were forced to retreat toward Cassville. Colonel Standish rode into the foe thinking they were part of Price's forces and was captured. About this time, the Third Louisiana regiment charged Sigel's forces with fixed bayonets and captured his battery and with the assistance of Texas and Arkansas troops put him in full flight. Up to this time we were between the fire of Sigel in our rear and [Nathaniel] Lyon in our front. For seven mortal hours we struggled with Lyon's advancing columns and Wilson Creek flowed colored with the blood of as fine a body of men as ever met in opposing columns.

It would take many of your valuable columns to tell of the heroic deeds that were performed there that hot August day. I fought with Champion through the battle after my horse was slain and received honorable mention in my General's report.

After the battle was over, the Captain detailed me with a score of others to hunt up our dead and collect them for burial. It was then that I saw the remains of the beautiful dapple-gray ridden by Gen. Lyon, the gift of D. A. January of St. Louis. He was a beautiful charger and has been immortalized with his master in painting and in song. I have often read "the rivers ran with blood" but I came near seeing it at Wilson Creek. Bleeding men and horses sought the creek that day and in many places the stream was red with blood of friend and foe. I was never in but one hotter fight in my four years' service and some day I may tell you of that.

R. E. Young

JOHN S. MARMADUKE

THE MISSOURI STATE TRIBUNE, SATURDAY EVENING NOVEMBER 24, 1900
PAGES 4 - 5

(Editor's note: The following letter was one of two reminiscences included in an article honoring John Sappington Marmaduke. The other reminiscence was written by E. W. Stephens)

To the Editor of the State Tribune:

In visiting the beautiful monument to the memory of the late Governor Marmaduke, many incidents of his eventful life that come to my personal knowledge came rushing into my mind.

My first acquaintance with Gen. Marmaduke was in this city in May 1861. He had come to this town with a company from Saline county, whether as an officer or private I do not now remember. Gen. M. M. Parsons was in command of the State troops at this place and this company from Saline county of which I speak was a part of his brigade. There were several detached companies here from various parts of the state and Gen. Parsons ordered them to form a regiment and elect regimental officers.

The company from Saline was among the members. The several officers of the companies referred to met in the building on the southwest corner of Broadway and High streets recently used as a voting place. After a tempestuous and somewhat drawn out session it was reported to Gen. Parsons that they were unable to agree on a Colonel. The messenger, who was Col. [Richard] Gains[*] of Parsons' staff, said if John Marmaduke was not so modest, he could easily be elected. Gen. Parsons replied: "He is the solution of the problem. Tell the officers in my opinion he is the best qualified man they can find." Gen. Marmaduke at the out-break of the war was a lieutenant of engineers in the U. S. army under Gen. Henry in the West.[**] When hostilities between the States began, he believed in state sovereignty and resigned his position in the U. S. army and offered his services to his state by enlisting in a company from his native county. In a few

[*] Col. Richard Gaines
[**] Marmaduke was a Second Lieutenant in the 7th U. S. Infantry Regiment; General William S. Harney commanded the Department of the West

JOHN SAPPINGTON MARMADUKE
MAJOR GENERAL C. S. A.
MISSOURI GOVERNOR 1884-87

days after he was elected colonel, his regiment was ordered to Boonville. He was in immediate command of Parson's brigade when the first battle of Boonville was fought. General Parsons didn't arrive until the forces had been repulsed and were in full retreat.

After this battle I lost personal sight of General Marmaduke until while we were in fortified camp at Little Rock after our retreat from Helena, some time in the fall of '63. One morning a little before sunrise while I was on guard on one of the bastions of our breastworks, a cavalcade of officers passed out of our fortifications by order of the officer of the guard. I noticed that one of them was General Marmaduke. They were not gone long until they returned. Soon after, an ambulance passed out and returned with the mortal remains of General [Lucius Marsh] Walker of one of the Arkansas brigades. General Marmaduke had killed him in a duel. The duel grew out of a misunderstanding between the two generals in an engagement with the enemy a few days before. As intimate as I became with General Marmaduke in after years, being his constant attendant as physician and friend and sleeping with him more than a score of times, he never alluded directly or indirectly to this duel. One of General Marmaduke's characteristics was to seldom speak of his prowess in arms.

No more fearless man ever lived when [Marmaduke] believed he was right and no man or combination of men could induce [Marmaduke] to do what he thought was wrong. I never saw the general under fire but once. Not being a member of his immediate command, I may say I never met him but once in battle. It was at the battle of Jenkin's Ferry. Our battery, Third Missouri commanded by Captain [Alexander A.] Lesueur, was in action alongside of a bayou and in about as hot a place as one could well imagine. It was raining and the water on the ground was from ankle to half leg deep. There was such a fog, together with smoke of [the] battle, that one could hardly see twenty paces in front. We knew the enemy were in strong force in front of us by the whistling of the bullets about our ears and by the dead, sad, wounded men and horses on every side. I don't remember how long we had been in action when a field officer galloped up and asked who commanded the battery. I recognized General Marmaduke. We pointed to Captain Lesueur. He rode up to him and said: "This battery is too far advanced. The enemy are out flanking you on the left. Fall back and take a position more tenable."

As he passed our gun going to another part of the field, I saw his spur on the left foot drop to the ground. A bullet had cut the strap when it passed under the foot. Several years after at Governor [John S.] Phelps' inauguration ball, I related this story to General Marmaduke and he said he remembered losing his spur that day but he never knew when or how.

As proof of what a considerate general he was for the safety of his troops, as we went out of that trap we met a section of artillery going into it. By this time Marmaduke was in some other portion of the field. The boys jeered us for falling back and moved forward to the position we had occupied. Soon after, Lon Boyle, a boy raised partly in Jefferson City and who belonged to the battery that took our place, came limping to us in full retreat and told us that the battery had been captured and he and one other were all that escaped. After the battle, in passing over the field hunting our dead and wounded, we found nearly all the members of the battery referred to dead [and] lying about where [our] guns had stood. Most of them had been knocked in the head with the butts of muskets by the negro troops who had outflanked and captured them.

Most of my knowledge of General Marmaduke was obtained while he was governor. In his first campaign, I met him on the Madison House steps and putting his hand on my shoulder, he said: "Here is a man that is for me for governor." I replied: "I would have been had I known you would be a candidate before I pledged my support to Hockaday." He replied: "Be always true to your word." A singular incident occurred while this contest was on. I had written him and Hockaday to make my house their homes while the convention was in session and while they both had headquarters at the Madison, both sought my house as a retreat from the worries of the campaign.

After Marmaduke had been elected governor and a few days before his inauguration was to take place, he was taken with a severe nose bleeding in the City of St. Louis. He was to be inaugurated on Monday the 12th of January at noon. On Sunday the 11th, his nose was still bleeding and he was very weak. His brothers and friends wanted him to give up coming to Jefferson City and be inaugurated by proxy. He was not to be deterred from his purpose to be inaugurated at the capitol as prescribed by law and said: "I will go to Jefferson City and have the ceremony performed where the law appoints if I die in my boots." Doctors told him he must not think of going. Sunday evening late, he told his private secretary, Colonel [Van Court] Yantis, to charter a car for Jefferson City, saying: "I know a doctor in Jefferson City that will advise me to be inaugurated in due form and will moreover put me in a condition to go through the trial." [Colonel Yantis] at once telegraphed that doctor [Dr. R. E. Young] to meet him at the train with a carriage.

About daylight, the doctor was there with a closed carriage and took him from the train to his own house where the good wife had provided to receive him. At 11:30 a.m. of the 12th the doctor took him in a closed carriage to the capitol and after the inauguration, bundled him back to bed where he kept him until he was sufficiently recovered to go to the mansion. Ever after he was unwilling to go far away from that doctor.

My relations with Governor Marmaduke during the three years he was governor were of the most confidential character. I always found him upright in all his dealings with the people. Once when a member of his official family had arranged to take a trip through Old Mexico as the guest of the Missouri Pacific railroad and had invited quite a number of friends to accompany him, he found that he had reckoned without first consulting his chief. When the governor heard of it, he called him into his presence and told him: "You cannot accept that courtesy from the railroad while you are a part of my official family." Pointing to me, he said: "The doctor can go and take his friends if he likes for he has no state relations with me. He is only my medical advisor." The gentleman spoken to was sorely disappointed for he had planned a gorgeous time. The governor was right and the railroad company did not care to invite the doctor.

In the great strike of 1885, he was begged on every side to call out the militia and at one time it looked like he would have to do it. He ordered the militia to camp at Centretown within striking distance of Sedalia, the great railroad center of the State. He believed in the people governing by the means provided by the civil authorities if possible and in using the militia arm of the State only when it could not be avoided. He was a Democrat to the core and not one merely for the purpose of getting office.

There are many incidents connected with my association with Governor Marmaduke that would be interesting to the public. One or two will suffice for this writing. When the great cattle plague of pleura-pneumonia threatened the great cattle interests of the State, a convention of cattlemen of the State assembled in his office to induce him to convene the Legislature to appropriate funds sufficient to have all the cattle in the infected districts killed. The governor invited me to be present. On the way to the capitol, I fell in with a noted lawyer who had been attorney-general of the State. He remarked to me that it was a pity a man of Marmaduke's natural and acquired ability was unable to make a speech. During the meeting, this lawyer made a legal argument in favor of the calling of the Legislature. Many others made strong appeals along the same lines.

After they were all through, the governor asked for further time to consider the matter but everyone was strong of the opinion that no time ought to be lost. An old gentleman who had known him from boyhood walked up to him and said: "John, you must decide now. The cattle of the State are dying by thousands." Arising and stretching himself to his full height, he began and in a speech of ten minutes he not only convinced the council that he would not convene the Legislature, but the large majority that it was not to the best interests of the taxpayers to do so. On our return, my lawyer friend said to me: "Marmaduke made the most forceful and convincing speech in ten minutes I ever heard."

Once when he was sick and I was at his bedside, one of the judges of the supreme court called to argue with him why he should commute the sentence of death to life imprisonment.

Two men had jointly committed the murder, a very cold-blooded one. The younger man, by the evidence, was the leader and instigator of the crime. There had been a great effort to commute the sentence of the younger man now advocated by the judge of the supreme court. At last Marmaduke yielded and sent for his private secretary to make out the papers. When he came, Marmaduke asked him if he had prepared the papers for commutation of the sentence of the older man in the joint crime. The secretary said: "Governor, no one has asked for commutation of sentence for the older man, it seems to me you ought to wait until some effort at least has been made by the community on his behalf." He replied, his eyes flashing with emotion: "I will never allow one man, who was less guilty in joint crime, to hang when the guilty one goes with a less punishment."

No man could make John Marmaduke do wrong in office if he saw it, nor could all the people in the world keep him from doing the right as he saw it. The people of Jefferson City ought never to forget

Governor Marmaduke. They ought to teach their children, generation after generation, to revere his name.

Once when I was attending him in his sickness, he said to me: "I am about to write my message to the Legislature and I am going to recommend that they submit a proposition to the people to settle where the permanent seat of government in this State shall be so that a capitol may be built commensurate with the wealth and prominence of Missouri." I loved my native city and I loved Marmaduke and I knew he would do what he thought was right so I set to work to convince him that the people had settled the question time and again. My labors were not in vain for one day after a long discussion of the subject, he said: "You have convinced me and I am going to treat the subject as settled and recommend an appropriation to improve the present capitol and settle the matter as far as I am able. This was the movement that largely contributed to the 153[illegible] majority that finally settled the matter as far as the people are concerned.

One more thought and I will conclude the subject that always has and always will interest me - Marmaduke's memory. The thought is this: That there ought to be inscribed on Marmaduke's monument: *John Marmaduke Believed in God and the People.*

                                                        R. E. Young

BORN IN SALINE CO., MO. MARCH 14, 1833,
YALE COLLEGE THREE YEARS,
HARVARD COLLEGE ONE YEAR.
GRADUATE OF WEST POINT MILITARY ACADEMY.
LIEUTENANT IN THE UNITED STATES ARMY.
CAPTAIN AND COLONEL, MO. STATE GUARD.
BRIGADIER GENERAL AND MAJOR GENERAL,
CONFEDERATE STATES ARMY.
SECRETARY STATE BOARD OF AGRICULTURE.
RAILROAD COMMISSIONER OF MO.
AND DIED WHILE GOVERNOR OF MISSOURI,
DEC. 28, 1887.
He was fearless AND *incorruptible*[*]

---

[*] Inscription on John S. Marmaduke's monument, Woodland Cemetery, Jefferson City

FROM 1848 TO 1851
SOMETHING INTERESTING OF JEFFERSON CITY
AT THIS TIME

THE MISSOURI STATE TRIBUNE, SATURDAY EVENING DECEMBER 1, 1900
PAGE 2, COLUMNS 3-4

To the Editor of the State Tribune:

Mrs. Lynn's select school for young girls and small boys was well patronized by the people of Jefferson City. She was a lady of more than ordinary mental power and for the age in which she lived [was] well educated and refined. She had a son, Duncan Lynn, who at the time of which I write was at a medical college in Virginia. He taught school awhile in Jefferson City and the writer was one of his pupils. The boys did not like him but that was no evidence [that] he was not a good teacher.

Mrs. Lynn had a nephew named Nathaniel and I doubt if he was exactly like his scriptural namesake: "without guilt." I used to be his boon companion and what mischief he, Nat Hough, and myself could not do in a day was simply what we three could not think of. We were positively forbidden to go swimming in the river. We were allowed to go in Miller's creek. So on Saturday, we would start away from home in that direction in the swimming season and in those times it came as early as the latter part of March or the 1st of April. When fairly out of sight, we would beat around to the mouth of Big or Ware's creek where the Missouri Pacific railroad bridge spans that stream and swim down to the penitentiary landing. When Nat Lynn learned to swim, I do not know. Nat Hough and I would carry his clothes and run along the bank of the river.

One day when the river was high, we found a flatboat anchored above the prison warehouse. You could jump off the end of this boat that was out in the stream and the swift current would wash you in the door of the warehouse which was some distance out in the river. The warehouse itself was in the water some distance. As the current washed you in at the end door, it carried you out at the lower side door where the water was only a few inches in depth. Nat Lynn persuaded Nat Hough and I that we could keep from going in that end of the warehouse and out of the side door if we wanted to. So we jumped off the end of the flatboat and trying to swim under Nat Lynn's instructions, went whistling through the end door and out the side. After a half day of this kind of practice, we learned to swim. Then we drew straws who should carry the clothes when we would swim from Ware's creek to the prison. It was not long until George Roots[*] and [Eli] Bass McHenry joined our party in the swimming business. Ernest Cordell was soon added and we were a half dozen hard to beat.

When we did not get whipped at school, we got it at home and sometimes at both places. In the summertime we would get a skiff, either borrowing with leave or without leave, just as circumstances indicated. Then we would row over to the bar in front of town and play in the water and in the sand. One day my father spied me from the roof of a house he was shingling and when I came up to go home with him, he suddenly-like asked me if I was in that skiff that went over to the bar. Somehow I caught on to the fact that he knew I had. Bracing myself up, I answered: "Yes, sir." Well, he had whipped me for disobedience before and here it was again. He just changed the mode of punishment by locking me up in a closet where he kept his tools and went off and left me intending to come back and let me out after he thought I was sufficiently punished. By some means, he forgot the incident and when he went home to supper, mother asked him if he had seen me uptown. He did not lose any time in going after me for he was a tender, kind-hearted man. I was tired when he locked me up and soon fell asleep and had not wakened when he came after me and was surprised to find it was dark. When we got home, I would not have swapped places with him for mother didn't say a thing to him. I was the youngest child and only boy so you may know mother and I were friends.

Just beyond the Lynn house on Water street and about where the waiting room of our present depot building now stands was a three-story brick building intended for a warehouse. There had been an attempt to change the river wharf or landing from the foot of Jefferson street to that of Monroe street. The effort failed and the building was never completed further than putting it under roof. Beyond this, a hundred feet or less, was the steam sawmill owned and operated by

[*] Rootes

Capt. Rodgers.* Logs were floated down the river near the mill and drawn by a tram-way out of the river up to the mill. Of the time I am writing, this sawmill did a thriving business but when the railroad came, the warehouse and mill both gave up the ghost, so to speak.

On Monroe street near Water, Squire Jason Harrison lived. He was a justice of the peace, in those days called squire. He afterwards became judge of the Circuit court. No better citizen or officer ever honored the county with his services. He was noted for his quiet demeanor and sturdy character. If he ever had any children, I never knew them.

A little further east on Water street was the Bohn mansion. I do not remember much of the Bohn family except that Al was a river pilot and Miss Sallie Bohn was what was called an "old maid" in those days. Miss Sallie was so well and favorably known in Jefferson City that when in after years she married Mr. Manchester, he told a friend that he had lost his identity and was only known as Miss Sallie Bohn's husband.

R. E. Young

---

* Rogers

GEN. G. A. PARSONS

THE MISSOURI STATE TRIBUNE, SATURDAY EVENING DECEMBER 15, 1900
PAGE 1, COLUMNS 5-6

To the Editor of the State Tribune:

Water street was not graded in the years of which I write beyond the Cordell residence. *Ne plus ultra* could have been truthfully written on it. Let us leave the street at the intersection of Jackson street and travel south as far as Main. Only one two-story frame house will be encountered. It is situated on the east side of the street and is occupied by the family of Gen. [Gustavus] A. Parsons. He was a portly gentleman of the southern type hailing from Virginia and proud of a relationship to Thomas Jefferson. When he came to Jefferson City, he was a brick mason. When I knew him, he had been a general in the Mormon War on Governor [Lilburn W.] Boggs' staff and was county and circuit clerk of Cole county. He was one of the most prominent characters of his time. Many people now living in Jefferson City knew him personally. When I first knew him, he was what was known as an anti-Benton Democrat and was one of the most popular men living in the county. Men's affinity for Gen. G. A. Parsons was something wonderful. He was bold and ready on any occasion to assert himself, whether in religion or politics. He was affable in his manners and had a kind greeting for all. In anger he was not choice in his language and his expletives were simple but quite forceful. One of them I shall never forget and I do not remember ever to have heard anyone else use it. It was "dod blast." When he applied it, he was thoroughly in earnest. It was said of him, that once when on a long hunt of which he was very fond, that a "bully" came into the camp and began to make a disturbance. Gen. Parsons politely told him to go away. He persisted in his efforts to raise a row when the General exclaimed: "Dod blast you! I will whip the hide off you!" And when the fray was over, those who saw it said the General came close to verifying his threat.

No man could ever beat him for county and circuit clerk until he was disfranchised by the Civil War and as soon as he was enfranchised, he was again elected and died in office. So great was his power over men that his mere presence easily made him the leader.

MOSBY MONROE PARSONS

His oldest son was General M. M. Parsons of the Confederate army. More of him anon.

Gen. G. A. Parsons' house was the home of any farmer that choose to make it so. When he invited a farmer home to dinner, he meant for him to come and invited him in such a manner that the farmer felt like he would offend if he did not accept. It no doubt was pretty hard for Mrs. Parsons but if she ever thought so no one knew it. It seemed like she always expected company for she always appeared prepared. Her name was Patience and she seemed the very personification of the name.

The General had a large family [and] some of them died before my recollection. I will here only speak of two daughters, Mildred and July. They were fast friends of my two elder sisters, Mary and Josephine. I doubt in those years if you could ever see one of those girls without seeing the other three. When they were not at our house, they were at Gen. Parsons'. I was the small boy in the scene and when I was not running errands for them, I was hatching and carrying out some scheme that made them wish I was in Halifax. Mildred Parsons and Mary Young were of an age and old enough to have beaus. Julia Parsons and Josephine Young were at that age when girls are most fond of each other but being near the age of the other two, were often required to be in the party as a kind of brake. The parents of both parties felt like things would be more in accordance with the proprieties if the younger girls never kept in the parties, picnics, and other gatherings. The beaux, as I remember them, in those days were Duncan Lynn, Clay and Eph Ewing, Green Berry, Christy Watson, Ed. Cordell, Lucius Kerr, Billy Miller, Billy Wells and Sam Owens. Of course there were others but I do not now call them to mind.

The enjoyment of the young people was very much the same as now. Horseback riding was very much in vogue in those days and parties of young ladies and gentlemen would frequently have riding parties to the country for picnicking or fishing. I do not now remember if I ever saw a young lady and a gentleman buggy riding and I know the parents of the girls I have named above would not have tolerated their daughters buggy riding with gentlemen after sundown. But those were simple people who lived in Jefferson City then. They did not believe many things that are done nowadays were right. They abhorred long engagements between marriageable young people and married people did not attend dancing parties or other gatherings of the single people.

Speaking of parties reminds me of the custom among the negroes of grooming the young gentleman's horse and that of the young lady who was to accompany him. When the party returned, if the young gentleman did not put a quarter in the "boy's" hand who took the horses to hitch, he at once fell into disfavor and as soon as the "boy" could see his young mistress after the gentleman was gone, some such a conversation as this would occur: "Say, Miss, I wouldn't have dat man; he's nothing but poo' white trash; never saw what his money looked like." If the negro was a little aged, the young gallant could make himself solid by giving the "ole man" a dram in addition to the quarter. "I tell you what, Miss, dat's de man fo' you; he don't care about a little money."

The young people in those days would get up dancing parties in the country and go in hacks or carriages and [after] dancing all night return[ed] in the early morning to the city or if it was to [sic] far out, return[ed] in the afternoon. The people had open fireplaces and the crackling fire from the logs heaped up in the chimney place made cheerful, comforting music. The young people danced until they joined the church and then quit or got turned out of the church.

R. E. Young

THE LONG AGO
THE OLD THESPIAN SOCIETY OF JEFFERSON CITY

THE MISSOURI STATE TRIBUNE, SATURDAY EVENING DECEMBER 22, 1900
PAGE 1, COLUMN 6; PAGE 8, COLUMN 1

To the Editor of the State Tribune:

In my last communication, I spoke of Gen. M. M. Parsons as the oldest son of Gen. G. A. Parsons. When I first remember Gen. M. M. Parsons, he was a practicing lawyer at the bar in this city. He was born in Virginia and came with his father to this State in 1836 or 1837. He obtained most of his education in St. Charles but he was largely a self-educated man. He told me of his early trials [and] how he worked about his father's brickyard to obtain money enough to go to St. Charles to put some finishing touches on his meager education. I think he read law with Judge Morrow who lived about where Sam Sone now lives, just west of the city limits. In 1846, he enlisted a company which was a part of the celebrated [Alexander W.] Doniphan's regiment from this State. He was in the battle[s] of Chihuahua and Sacramento and acquitted himself with credit to his regiment. He was a brave man, whether on the battlefield or at the bar. He was never known to flinch, whether in a passage at arms or in a heated debate. He was over six feet tall, muscular, and erect in carriage. No handsomer man ever walked the streets of Jefferson City in his day. Quiet in manner, fierce in anger, and determined in purpose.

He was a dangerous man to move to passion. Once in a heated argument before a jury, he said some severe things about a witness. After leaving the court, the witness called him to a personal account. It resulted in a rough and tumble fight, a thing very common in those days. When the fight was over, Parsons was but slightly hurt [and] they had to put the other man to bed. After he recovered, he met Parsons one day on the street and offering him his hand, said: "It was that ____ left hand of yours that did the work for me."

Capt. Monroe Parsons, as he was called in those days, was fond of theatricals and was at the head of a home company called the Thespian Society. The first acting I ever saw was done by this company. The play was Hamlet and Capt. Parsons was the Hamlet. I have heard the older people who were old enough to appreciate good acting say that the company was a good one. They played in the old circuit court room which many now living in Jefferson City will remember. In fact, almost every kind of entertainment was in this court room. My first appearance in public was there in "The boy stood on the burning deck," etc.

Some amusing scenes occurred in this old room, one of which comes vividly to mind. Mesmerism was the rage of that time and some performer was giving an exhibition of his powers. All the youth that could be gotten to come forward occupied a bench facing the audience. There was Cal. Gunn, George Steele, Frank Anderson, Sam Owens, Warwick Hough and Jim Blevins that I now remember. They were required to look at a copper disk about the size of an old fashioned cup plate with a bright spot in the center. They were told to look at this bright spot until the professor (these kind of fakes were called professor then as now) told them to quit. After 15 or 20 minutes of this steady looking, he took the discs away and began to exercise his powers of mesmerism over them. The entire class, with the exception of Jim Blevins, proved to be unmanageable by the professor and were dismissed with the assertion that they did not look intensely enough. Jim appeared to be in his powers. He made him do anything he wanted him to do, such as passing an empty plate to the young ladies and asking one if she would have a bouquet or some cake, candy, or trinket. Jim seemed to believe these things were on the plate. I don't think after that night Jim could have waited on a young lady in this town. Women, as a rule, do not care much for men they think mentally or physically inferior to the general average. In those days the girls loved the young gallant best who would dare the most along our line.

Many a forensic battle was fought in that old court room, now no more. Messrs. Napton, Scott, Hayden, Edwards, Gardenhire, Wells, Todd, and Parsons measured with each other as lawyers and debaters. Many amusing incidents occurred then besides witty repartees. I do not pretend to remember all the leading lawyers of those days but some of them were left until my time and some of the incidents interesting occurred under my observation and others were told me by my father and Capt. Parsons, Gen. Edwards and others. Some of these I will try to relate in my next.

R. E. Young

LEGAL TILTS
SOME INCIDENTS OF THE PRACTICE OF LAW

THE MISSOURI STATE TRIBUNE, SATURDAY EVENING DECEMBER 29, 1900
PAGE 1, COLUMNS 1-2

To the Editor of the State Tribune:

I promised in my last communication to relate a few of the incidents that occurred in the old Circuit Court room about fifty years ago. These stories were mostly related to me by my father, Gen. Parsons, and Judge Edwards.

Judge Todd, a very portly and jolly man, was on the bench and Judge Napton and Mr. Hayden were pitted against each other in the case. The trial had been a tedious one and extended over several days. When before the jury, both became very much in earnest. Napton was a young lawyer fresh from the University of Virginia and one of the best educated men at that time in the State. He was tall and lithe in form and altogether very handsome. Hayden was medium in height and rather corpulent. He wore a wig with a queue that extended down his back and was tied with a black ribbon. One of his eyes was defective from some injury that occurred early in life. In the debate before the jury, Mr. Hayden alluded to his friend Napton as an inexperienced youth who, although splendidly educated, had much to learn that was practical in life. He laid great stress on the fine and handsome appearance of his young friend and said it was a pity that he had been sent into the Western wilds to contend with the adverse circumstances that was incident to the imperfect condition of society. It would have been better to have kept him where men wore swallow-tail coats, silk hats, and kid gloves. Napton at once saw the force this would have with the sturdy jury before him - rough in exterior themselves, they had little patience with what was then called a dandy - now called a dude. After Napton had made his argument, which was a forceful one, he concluded somewhat in the following strain. He said he knew full well that he had committed the crime of being a young man. But for this, he did not feel that he was to blame. No doubt, at some remote period, his friend Hayden had committed the same offense. But he said, what astonished him was that those who had the early care of his friend Hayden did not realize to what eminence he in after life would attain. Why, said he, they took indifferent care of him, allowed him to run at large with the little niggers, and that one had pushed him in the fire and burned all the hair off his head and another had hooked his eye out with pot-hooks. The jury and Judge Todd were so concussed with laughter at Hayden's expense that it was several minutes before the judge could control himself sufficiently to command the sheriff to restore order in the court. It was said that Hayden was ever after careful in his personal illusions to Napton.

Whether it was after this incident or before, I do not now remember but I think it was before. Judge Todd made one ruling that was adverse to Napton's contention when Napton, in a loud and forceful manner, took issue with the court. In his remarks, he severely criticized Judge Todd's opinion and in his effort displayed great erudition and power as a lawyer and debater. After he was through, Judge Todd complimented him highly and then said: "Mr. Napton, when your power to practically apply the law shall equal your acquired and natural abilities, you will be a master in the profession."

In speaking of this incident to my father in after years, Judge Napton said nothing ever did him so much good as that gentle rebuke from Judge Todd. Judge Todd was full of humor and was always wide awake to anything ridiculous. Once, when an attorney was questioning a witness with a small table between him and the witness, the attorney said to the witness: "Stop, now; only tell what you know." The witness was one William J. Kelly of Moniteau county, a gentleman of quick wit and undaunted courage. Mr. Kelly, quick as a flash, struck the attorney, knocking him and the table over on the floor. Judge Todd was so full of laughter that he had to turn his back to the scene while his fat sides shook with compulsive efforts to restrain himself. The attorney picked himself up and remarked to the court for a redress of his advance. By this time, Judge Todd had turned back facing the lawyer and quietly remarked to the attorney to go on with the redress.

Once, just as Judge Todd had adjourned his court, a fight occurred at the side door. General James L. Minor, the attorney-general of Gov. Boggs' administration, had attacked my father [by] drawing a dirk on him. My father was coming out of the court room and General Minor was coming in. My father was a very active man and his muscles were well under command, being hardened by work at his trade. An empty barrel stood just outside the door and the top of it

THE OLD COURTHOUSE

was flush with the top step going down into the yard. The barrel was used for putting ashes in but was empty at the time. My father knocked Minor's arm up, sending the dirk out into the yard and with the other knocked Minor in the ash barrel. Before he could follow it up, Judge Scott of the Supreme Court grabbed Father from behind with both arms around him. Judge Todd exclaimed: "Hold him Scott till Minor gets out of the barrel." Father then said, seeing he was in the hands of his friends: "Maybe you had better hold the other man."

The difficulty grew out of a funny piece of rhyme on Gov. Boggs' administration which General Minor accused my father of publishing. They fought duels in those days and when General Minor was finally extricated from the barrel, he said: "My friend will call on you Colonel." My father was judge advocate of a militia regiment or brigade, I do not now remember, they mustered in those days. I do not know how the matter was arranged but no duel was fought and in after years no two men were better friends than General Minor and my father. Judge Scott and Judge Todd were both friends of my father and Scott asked Father: "What would you have done to me if you could have gotten loose?" Before father could answer, Todd said: "Why, he would have whipped you till your wife wouldn't know you."

R. E. Young

JOHN SMITH R.[*]

RECOLLECTIONS OF THIS FAMOUS BELLIGERENT

THE MISSOURI STATE TRIBUNE, SATURDAY EVENING JANUARY 12, 1901
PAGE 2, COLUMNS 5-6

FROM 1848 TO 1851

To the Editor of the State Tribune:

Among the celebrities that used to meet in the old circuit court room was Judge R. A. Wells of the United States district court. Judge Wells held court at two places in Missouri, one here and the other in St. Louis. I believe there was but one district of the whole state at that time but I am not certain of it. The Judge was tall and slender in person and went well dressed in black broadcloth and silk hat. He was very polite in manner, unless aroused, when he displayed great temper and irritability. He had a peculiarity when talking to a friend on the street that I do not remember ever to have seen in anyone else. In these street talks, he would nudge you and turn you around as if to view you in another light. He was known to frequently nudge a friend half a square from where the conversation began. To those he did not regard as special friends, he would only bow and pass on.

He was a brave man and held the distinction of being the only man in the state who ever antagonized the notorious John Smith R. and came out of it with a whole hide. The incident occurred some time in the thirties when Judge Wells was a young man assisting Major Barcroft in surveying the state. They had passed through John Smith R.'s land and incurred his displeasure. Smith met them as they were passing off the premises and in his blustering manner demanded why they dared to pass through his premises without his permission. Major Barcroft, the state surveyor, attempted to make some explanation when Smith R. as he was called, became insulting in his language. Young Wells stepped quickly forward and handed Smith R. his card exclaiming: "We thought we were on a gentleman's premises." This act resulted in the exchange of cards and the selection of friends to represent the principals. The duel did not come off for some reason unknown to the writer. But it was a bold act on the part of young

---

[*] actually John Smith T.

Wells, because John Smith R. was known from one end of the state to the other as a desperate man; his friends claiming for him that he had killed more than a dozen men in duello. He had appended the letter R to his name to distinguish him from any of the other numerous John Smiths.

In this connection, I remember an interesting incident that occurred in this city in a very early day in which the late General Rollins of Columbia and this same John Smith R. figured as principals. At a point nearly opposite the present manor on Madison street stood the once famous hostelry known as the Rising Sun kept by Major Basey.* Rollins had just come to the State from Kentucky and was visiting the capital for the first time. Of course he put up at the Rising Sun and being a gentlemanly-appearing man, Maj. Basey* gave him the best quarters he had vacant at the time. John Smith R. was stopping at the hotel at the same time. Rollins had heard of Smith R. and of his desperate character but did not know that he was at that time in the city. It was Smith R.'s custom to take a negro boy with him who carried a double-barreled shotgun. Smith R. himself carried two Derringer pistols in his belt. It was before the days of revolvers. To the hotels, then as now, a bar was attached where the men could refresh themselves; in signification of, the sign read: *"Rising Sun Inn: Refreshments for Man and Beast."* Rollins noticed a shotgun sitting in the corner of the office and had also noticed that a likely negro boy sat near the gun but paid no particular attention to either the negro or the gun. Presently, a stout and somewhat burly appearing gentleman entered the office and walking to the open fireplace, turned his back to the fire and his face toward Rollins. It was customary in those days for men to speak to each other without any formal introduction and so a conversation soon sprang up. After they had conversed for a short time, Smith R. asked Rollins to accompany him to the bar and join him in liquid refreshments. Rollins asked to be excused, pleading that it was his habit to confine himself to water and coffee as beverages. Smith R. at once became indignant and said: "Do you know with whom you refuse to drink socially?" Rollins politely said he did not and that he did not wish to give offense by his refusal but must insist that he would not drink. "You will drink," said Smith R., "or give me the personal satisfaction for the insult offered by refusing to drink

---
* Basye

socially with John Smith R." At the sound of the name, Rollins noticed that the negro in the corner got up and shouldered the gun. There seemed no way to Rollins out of the difficulty but to submit or fight. There appeared too much against him to think of fighting and so he selected the former in his bland and pleasing manner and apologized for refusing to drink with such distinguished a gentleman as John Smith R. and asked his host to lead on. When they arrived at the bar, which was joining the "office," Smith R. said: "What will you drink?" Rollins replied he had no choice in liquors and would be pleased to take the same as his host. "Gins and whisky then," said Smith. Two gins and a bottle were placed upon the counter and Smith said: "We will drink like Virginia gentlemen." "How is that," replied Rollins. "Why," said Smith "you pour my drink and I'll pour yours." Rollins was at a loss to know what to do. If he poured Smith's glass full, he was afraid he would take umbrage and Smith R. would order the negro in the corner to shoot him with the shotgun and if he poured too little, the result would be the same. At last he acted and filled Smith's glass about half full; Smith R. then filled Rollins' glass to the top and they were the old-fashioned glasses holding at least as much again as those of this age. They touched glasses and returned to the office where the conversation about Missouri and her [illegible]esta was resumed. Rollins, being unused to liquor, soon found himself ground drunk. The last thing he remembered was Smith calling the landlord and requesting him to put his friend Rollins to bed. When he awoke next morning, he was happy to learn of Major Basey[*] that Smith had departed on the early stage coach for St. Louis.

When you consider what a reputation this man Smith R. had and his desperate deeds, you can appreciate Judge Wells' courage in handing him his card.

R. E. Young

---

[*] Basye

REMINISCENCES
DR. YOUNG CONTRIBUTES ANOTHER CHAPTER

THE MISSOURI STATE TRIBUNE, SATURDAY EVENING JANUARY 26, 1901
PAGE 1, COLUMNS 5-6

To the Editor of the State Tribune:

In my last communication, I made a digression from the purpose of my writing to tell an anecdote of Gen. Rollins in regard to Smith R. I now desire to return to reminiscences of my friend R. A. Wells. He was one of the most polished gentlemen that ever practiced in the old court house of Cole county. I am not positive as to his politics but think he was a Whig. I think he received his appointment in [President Zachary] Taylor's administration.

Once he was a candidate for judge of the circuit court of this district; that was before he was appointed to the Federal bench. He was beaten by a very close vote. Part of his district was on the east side of the Maries creek and the polling place was on the west side. On the election day, the Maries was very high and there were no bridges at that time over the stream. When the returns were all in, the judge attributed his defeat to the inability of his friends to get to the polling place. Some time afterward, he met a friend from that region and sought condolence from his friend by calling his attention to the fact that the Maries was not fordable on election day and that his friends could not reach the polls. His friend put his hand on the judge's shoulder, and remarked: "Judge, [you] didn't have a friend that didn't swim the Maries to vote for you. No, judge, there were too many Democrats." The judge liked to tell this story in after years when he heard someone trying to explain why he was defeated.

The judge concluded to buy a farm on the Osage and farm it by putting negroes on it. Some year or two after this, my father asked him how he was progressing in his farming venture. He replied: "Very well," he said, "but what troubles me is Lawyer Wells' has to pay too many of Farmer Wells' bills."

He owned many slaves but was a kind and indulgent master. He had a fine looking and able bodied man called Tim. One summer Tim concluded he would run out to keep from work. The judge supposed he had run off for good and did not hunt for him very much. He had two other faithful men, called Elias and Dick. One morning, after winter had set in in earnest, Tim appeared at the "quarters" and the judge was informed of the fact. He sent for him and Tim appeared in the judge's room and began to explain why he had been gone so long. He said that one of the skiffs belonging to the farm had broken from its mooring and he had been down the river hunting for it. The judge looked at the negro and pleasantly said: "That is very well Timothy, my boy. It will do to tell to Elias and Richard my boy but not to the judge. Go in the kitchen Timothy and get your breakfast and after you are through, I will give you h__l." After breakfast, the judge did not choose to remember that Tim had ever ran away. This became a saying among all the darkies of the country ever after when one of the members told a story: "It will do to tell to Elias and Dick but not to the judge."

Judge Wells' first wife was a Rector and by her he had three children, William, Mary, and Josephine. Mary became the wife of Capt. Parsons. For some reason unknown to anyone, the judge opposed the marriage and the parties eloped. It was a long time after their marriage before the judge became reconciled to the match. My father was a warm friend of both Wells and Parsons and by constant effort, got the judge to invite them to his house and the family relations were ostensibly resumed but the judge's pride was wounded and it left a sore that was hard to heal. When Capt. Parsons joined the rebels, it broke out afresh for the judge was an uncompromising Union man.

During the war, my father was arrested by the Union troops and thrown into prison for his supposed aid and sympathy to the rebels. Judge Wells knew the whole thing grew out of the fact that I was in the rebel army and had great sympathy for my father. The general in command notified my father that he intended to banish him. Father remembered the close relations that had always existed between Judge Wells and himself and knowing that he was on the Federal bench, sent for him. The judge informed father that, by the order of President Lincoln, he could choose the place of his punishment to any point north of the Potomac and Ohio rivers and east of the Mississippi. He also gave him a letter to Mr. Lincoln explaining the true status of the case. When the General in command learned that father intended to claim his rights under President Lincoln's order, he concluded to parole him instead of banishing him.

Judge Wells used to hold court here and in St. Louis. When the river was navigable, he went by boat but often he had to go by stage coach. In 1855, when the railroad was completed to this place, he was in St. Louis and was on that fatal train that plunged off the Gasconade bridge. After this, far as I know, he was never in another railroad car. He was superstitious of railroads and either went on a boat or by private overland conveyance. An anecdote was told of him, characteristic of his great politeness, the foundation of which occurred during the railroad accident referred to. In his car the stove had fallen on his hand and pinned it to the floor. The judge in some way held another passenger down so that he could not get up. The man, with deep and loud curses, demanded that the judge get off him and let him up. The judge, in that bland and polite manner peculiar to him, said: "I will only be too glad to do so if you can produce someone to take this stove off me."

At the time of which I write, Main street, as now, ended at the junction with Cherry street. The first house coming west now occupied by Steve Chapman and Jesse W. Henry was occupied by John C. Gordon. I do not remember him but think he was in some way connected to the penitentiary. But I remember very forcibly an incident that occurred at that house in which I was the chief actor. My father was building a house where the Warden's house [700 E. Main] now stands and I was playing about the premises. A friend of the family, Mrs. Wilburn was living with her brother, John C. Gordon. She gave me permission to eat all the raspberries and mulberries that I wanted. There was in that garden the finest English raspberries and white mulberries I ever saw. How many I ate I could never tell. It was in the cholera times of 1849 of which I will speak later on. When I went home to dinner, I wasn't a bit hungry, a rare condition for me. Along about 3 o'clock in the afternoon I was what my mother called a very sick child. Dr. [A.] M. Davison was sent for in great haste. Everybody thought I had the cholera. I say everybody [but] I don't know what the doctor thought. Soon after, he came and gave me some medicine and I will assure you it was the regular medicine given in the regular dose. It was not long until mother said: "Where on earth did you get those raspberries and mulberries?" When I told her, she said Mrs. Wilburn ought to have better sense than to turn me loose in a raspberry patch.

R. E. Young

THE LONG AGO
INTERESTING FACTS CONCERNING THE JEFFERSON CITY
THAT FLOURISHED IN THE EARLY FIFTIES

THE MISSOURI STATE TRIBUNE, SATURDAY EVENING FEBRUARY 2, 1901
PAGE 4, COLUMNS 3-4

To the Editor of the State Tribune:

The next house to that of John C. Gordon's on Main street was the one my father was building for Thomas Wilburn. He was one of the first merchant tailors of Jefferson City and did a thriving business until the gold fever of '49 broke out when he crossed the plains to the New Eldorado. Before he left, he engaged my father to construct the house of which I spoke. The house remained until in Marmaduke's administration when it was torn away and the present warden's house constructed in its stead. The Wilburns had three daughters who were playmates of my sisters. My earliest recollections are mixed up with my playing with these girls, making mud pies, playing with dolls, and other girlish sports. In 1851 or '53, Mr. Wilburn moved his family to California where I have heard the girls married happily.

The next house coming westward was a log structure weatherboarded and plastered on the inside. It stood about where my house now is. In fact, I tore it down to get room to build my present home. At the time of which I write, it was owned and occupied by John McCracken. The grounds of this house extended from Mrs. E. Ewings's residence to that of Mr. Claggett's including both. Mr. McCracken had on these grounds a fine garden and small orchard. We boys found occasion, frequently, to eat the cherries and plums in the summertime. One of the cherry trees remained some years after I bought that part of the grounds now occupied by my residence. A funny experience was had by my wife in regard to that cherry tree. One day a boy came to her and asked her if he might have some cherries that were still left after picking all that could be reached by means of a small step-ladder. She told him she was so glad he had come and asked her rather than steal them. She gave him a small bucket and told him if he would pick that full for her, he might have all that was left on the tree to eat or do what he chose to do in the matter.

She went away about her household duties. Some time after, thinking he had about finished, she went to get her bucketful as she supposed. What was her astonishment to behold neither boy nor bucket, empty nor full, was in sight. Neither was there any cherries on the tree. She thinks to this day that he was a very wicked boy. But she never was able to describe the boy and I doubt if she would have known him if she had met him.

I do not remember much about John McCracken except that he was a printer and I have been told he published a paper here called the *Metropolitan*. He had a boy called Bob. Bob McCracken was younger than our set but persisted in running with us and true to our savage natures, we made him suffer for his temerity. We had nothing against Bob but on account of his youthfulness, we were afraid he might "tell." I suppose the boys today of our then ages would call him a "kid." We called him a "booby." There is no better evidence that we are naturally savages as a race than the "small boy" is able to furnish. He has no mercy on his inferior brother and dogs and cats if they happen to get his ill will, give him no compunction of conscience for any suffering he may cause them.

Another incident causes me to remember John McCracken. We had a pony horse called "Kinderhook." He was a great pet with us children and would allow us to climb on his back until the hindmost one would fall off for want of room. Our mother often predicted that he would either paw us or kick us but he never did. He was valuable as a saddle horse, being able to go all the gaits. Women and children could ride him without fear but for some reason he was rather spirited when a man was on him. My father, being a practical man, concluded that he needed many things more than a family horse and as McCracken wanted him, father sold him. It was a long time before we children forgave Mr. McCracken for buying him and I fear many wicked wishes were made towards the innocent purchaser. I know I wanted "Kinderhook" to throw him every time I saw him riding him.

The next house west of McCracken's was a frame structure that stood where ex-Gov. [Lon V.] Stephens' Ivy Terrace is today. I do not remember who lived there at the time of which I write.

I will now, on account of the dedication of the new Methodist church, skip to the ground which it occupies. There was a house, partly frame and partly brick, owned by Henry Wegman. Henry was a German and one of the solid and reliable business men of Jefferson

City in those days. He was what was called in those days a dray-man. I have not seen a dray in many years like the one Henry Wegman used. It was a two-wheeled with shafts and two long skids extending from the rear of the body which was square or rectangular with standards instead of side boards. The skids extended some six or eight foot to the rear and were armed at the far ends with iron coverings. The skids had holes in them at regular intervals into which iron-bound standards could be placed. There were two of these iron standards to each dray. They were used for two purposes; one to insert at the rear part of the body of the dray to hold in loads and the other to insert in the skids to hold barrels and hogsheads while they were in the process of being loaded. The shafts of the dray were held on the horses by means of a chain and pack saddle such as they nowadays use in a cart. Generally, two horses were necessary for a dray; some [had], where the load required, three, four, or more all hitched tandem. Henry hauled freight from the landing at the foot of Jefferson street up to High and thence to the several stores in the town. He was a good natured man and liked the boys, generally, who would play all kinds of pranks on him, chiefly to hear his German way using English expletives. They would pull out the iron standards of his dray and let a barrel roll off and then scamper away. Woe unto them if they got in reach of his long "black snake whip." He would crack it around their bare legs, laugh at their calamity, and mock them when their fear came. But Henry did not hold a grudge and soon forgave the boys that teased him and let them ride when he had no load or when it was light.

R. E. Young

REMINISCENCES
GEN. JAMES L. MINOR'S REPLEVIN SUIT

THE MISSOURI STATE TRIBUNE, SATURDAY EVENING FEBRUARY 9, 1901
PAGE 1, COLUMNS 1-2

To the Editor of the State Tribune:

Just across the street from Ivy Terrace on the premises occupied by Dr. [Addison] Elston, lived the Widow Lisle. She was the widow of a prominent attorney, Dan Lisle. I never knew Mr. Lisle; he having died before I could remember. Mrs. Lisle had three daughters, Jane, Dollie, and Sue. In her youth, Miss Sue died. Jane and Dollie were twins and about my age. They were Presbyterians and went to the same Sunday School with my sisters and me. Mrs. Lisle was a great lover of flowers and always had a large variety. Flowers in those days were not used in the churches except in the Episcopal and Catholic. But the Presbyterian and Methodist churches gave entertainments for the benefit of their respective churches, then as now, and these were mostly held in the Senate chamber at the capitol. For these festivals, Mrs. Lisle and Mrs. Cordell generally furnished the flowers.

Miss Jane and Miss Dollie were my fast friends as a boy and our friendship lasted until I went away with the "Johnny Rebs." They were strong Union people and during the war a coldness sprang up between them and my people. I was far removed from the scene of their differences and did not enter into them. When I returned, the girls had married. Miss Jane became the wife of Hon. E. L. King and Miss Dollie the wife of Austin King, esq. Just across the street from Mrs. Lisle were some log houses. The ground is now occupied by Mrs. John W. Gordon's residence [429 E. Main]. These old houses had once been occupied by the Hon. Geo. Walker who was one of the early State Treasurers. He died before my day but I knew several of his family, especially Miss Rachel Walker who was for many years one of the noted characters of Jefferson City, dying at the ripe age of 84 years. Everyone that ever knew Miss Rachel was better for the acquaintance. She was one of the women who truly swept about doing good. These old log houses were vacant at the time of which I speak and furnished quarters, especially for us boys, to hold circuses in. For I assure you, the circus idea among boys was as rampant in the days of yore as in these days. We had not advanced to the device of street parades but we had clowns and acrobats galore. We had trick dogs and goats, just the same as the boys have now. I do not know how the boys of today manage their circuses but ours were most difficult to manage. In our efforts to have a good circus, every boy wanted to boss and generally after two or three rehearsals, we broke up in a sort of free for all fight.

The next house on Main street going west from the Walker corner was a frame and when I remember, it was occupied by the Abbotts. I only knew these people by name. I think the gentleman was a physician. Across the street from the Abbotts, in the house now occupied by Mrs. [Elizabeth] Dunscomb [420 E. Main], lived General James L. Minor. He was a prominent attorney when I first knew him. In after years, he was a successful farmer. He had been attorney-general in the Boggs administration. I have heard many anecdotes about General Minor as an attorney. One comes vividly to my recollection. In the Harrison campaign of 1840, a well-known citizen of Cole, known as "Uncle" Joel Melton, bet a gray mare against $50 that [William H.] Harrison would be defeated. After the election was over and "Uncle" Joel Melton had lost his mare and delivered her to the winner, someone told him that betting was illegal and he did not have to give her up. But the winner had the mare and refused to let "Uncle Joel" have her. So "Uncle Joel" consulted General Minor and he told him he thought a replevin suit would be successful. The suit was brought and a jury called and after a trial, "Uncle Joel" lost again. "Uncle Joel" had a habit of getting about "half shoaled over," to use a nautical phrase, when he came to town and the young men of the age of Pope Dorris, Shelton, Burch, Bill Lusk, Pope, Gordon, Ben[jamin W.] Winston, and Thad Boone would get him on a goods box and get him to make a speech!

After the trial, in which he lost his gray mare, the boys had him on an empty goods box making one of his random speeches when some on in the crowd said: "How about the gray mare Uncle Joel?" He shouted: "I never would have lost the gray mare but I employed Jim Minor to replevin her, and all he said to the jury was Chickerrak and of course, I lost her!"

With the family of General Minor lived my friend and chum, George Roots.* He was kin to the Minors but just how I do not remember. His sister, Miss Betty, was a young lady at the time of which I write, and was considered by all odds the belle of the place. She married a Southern gentleman and lives somewhere in Mississippi.

George and I were not only fast friends when boys but shared the same blanket in the rebel army. We often foraged together and as George was a good singer, we generally fared well. There is nothing that takes with the average girl like a soldier that can sing. Once upon a time, George and I struck a town where there was whisky. Whisky and a soldier take together about like a duck takes to water. Just how much we drank will never be known. However, we got to camp and to bed. Next morning after roll call, we compared notes and our conclusion was that we had about as brown a taste in our mouths as was possible. George had a piece of red velvet that I had often wanted him to divide with me to cover the cuffs of my coat which were badly worn. We were in the artillery service and our trimmings were red. The Confederate Government was not prodigal in furnishing clothing, or anything else for that matter, so that the soldier had to kind of look out for himself. George said there was just enough in the piece to make a vest and he would never part with it until he had an opportunity to have the vest made. After we had told each other how miserable we felt, George looked quizzically at me and said: "Bob, give me a drink for God's sake if you have one!" I replied: "I haven't any whisky; we drank it up yesterday." "He looked at me nercely [sic] and said: "You are a liar by the watch. You were never known to get drunk without saving enough to get sober on." "Well, George," I said, "how much of that red velvet would you give for a drink if I had one?" "All of it," he said. "D__n the vest anyhow." I told him I only wanted half of it and if he would come in the tent, where the other "boys" couldn't see us, I would try to find a drink if there was that much left. We found a pint in the bottle which I had carefully hid the night before and we were soon happy again. But we were careful to taper off gradually for we both knew there was no more to be had for love nor money."

After passing the Minor residence, the next one on the same side of the street was the one occupied by Mr. Perry Rader. It

---

* Rootes

belonged to the Widow Bay, a sister of E. B. Cordell, a gentleman named in these letters previously. Mr. Henry Cordell, Mrs. Bay's brother, lived in this house at the time of which I write and I think his sister lived with him. The children of both families were small and though I knew them in after years, I did not know them at this time.

Mrs. Henry Cordell was a pretty woman and very vivacious. When single, she was a Miss Mart. She had been heard to say that if she ever had three boys, she would call them Tom, Dick, and Harry as she had heard that expression all her life and had never seen the three together. When I remember her, she had all three, Tom, Dick, and Harry, and as bright and promising a trio as I ever saw.

Mr. Henry Cordell was a great favorite with my mother. He kept store for his brother Enos Cordell and had the unlimited confidence of everyone. He taught Sunday School in the Presbyterian Church and together with little Tom Miller sat on the front pew in the church and raised the tune which the preacher said when he gave out the hymn and was long meter, short meter, or difficult meter whichever it might be. Mr. P. T. Miller was called Little Tom not because he was particularly small but because he was not as large as his Uncle Tom Miller.

Mrs. Bay was a fine-looking lady and had many admirers but I believe she never married. When Gov. Bob Stewart was in the Mansion, she attended one of his receptions. He was a bachelor and passingly [sic] good looking. He appeared fond of the society of Mrs. Bay. Someone insisted that the governor join in the dance. He declined but was again and again urged to join in the dance. Finally, he consented and dancing with Mrs. Bay at the time, he said: "Well, lead on, I will trot out the Bay." It was said that she danced that set with him but would never speak to him afterwards.

R. E. Young

STORIES
OF PEOPLE AND EVENTS IN JEFFERSON CITY

THE MISSOURI STATE TRIBUNE, SATURDAY EVENING FEBRUARY 16, 1901
PAGE 1, COLUMNS 1-2

To the Editor of the State Tribune:

Just across the street from the stone house now occupied by Perry Rader [410 E. Main] was, at the time of which I am writing, some vacant lots which are now covered by the houses of Gen. McIntyre, Mrs. Cox, Wendell Straub, and the Methodist parsonage. These lots together with a log house on the alley in the rear of them belonged to "Uncle Billy" Hart, a colored man who had at one time belonged to the Hart Estate. "Uncle Billy," as every one called him, old and young, white and black, had been free many years when I knew him. Just how he obtained his freedom I do not know. When I first remember him, he owned the lots and the house of which I speak. "Uncle Billy" was the body servant of the supreme court which then consisted of Scott, Napton, and Leonard. "Uncle Billy" was frequently called the fourth member of the court and as he was nearly as white as the judges, many a rich joke was played upon the uninitiated by means of "Uncle Billy." In these days, the court met here, in St. Louis, and St. Joseph and "Uncle Billy" with the court attended to their personal comforts. There was only one of the judges who had as large a head as "Uncle Billy" - Judge Scott. "Uncle Billy" always wore one of the judge's cast-off hats and was very proud of it. "Uncle Billy" was very provident and died better off in this world's goods than many a one who served on the bench. I cannot pass on without mentioning "Uncle Billy's" wife, "Auntie Mariah." She was the unfailing friend of children, white and black. Many a time I have partaken of her hospitality and her sweet cakes were just better than anybody's. She had a daughter that in after years became noted as a nurse. And many a lady and more youngsters of today remember Auntie Bettie Mack. "Uncle Billy," in addition to waiting upon the supreme court, had a couple of teams hauling about town. I think he burned and hauled lime. He did not own slaves but he hired them from their white masters. I do not know what became of him while I was in the army.

There were no more houses on Main street until you came to about where the Christian Church now stands. Dr. Mills lived in a frame structure at about that point. I do not remember the doctor but he had a son, Thom, who belonged to the "gang" of boys I went with. Thom was a smooth sort of boy, went a little better dressed than the rest of us, and was not popular. We generally gave him the shake when we went on our exploits that were not to be talked of. My recollection is that the girls liked him and our mothers were apt to hold him up as a pattern. That kind of thing is fatal to the comfort of any boy among his fellows.

The next house after Dr. Mills' going west was on the lot now occupied by the Baptist Church. George W. Hough lived in it. Mr. Hough was a merchant all the time of which I write and had a store where the City Hotel saloon now is. The firm name was either *Hough & Stewart* or *Stewart & Hough*, I don't remember which. Mr. Hough had a most interesting family. Nathaniel, or "Nat" as we boys called him, was one of my constant companions and some years after, when he was killed by accidental explosion, there was not a boy who had ever known him that did not truly mourn his loss. There were three boys in the family besides "Nat." Warwick, who afterwards became judge of the supreme court and is now one of the judges in St. Louis, was much older than the rest of us boys and ran with another "gang." Charley, now a physician, and Arthur, a lawyer, were too young to go with "us." There were three or four daughters in the family but Laura, afterwards Mrs. Kaiser of St. Louis, was the only one I knew much. Mrs. Dr. Winston, the oldest daughter, still lives in Jefferson City. They lived just across Monroe street from where my parents lived.

We children were together every day. My sister Anna and Laura were chums. I don't know if "Nat" liked my sisters or not but I did not like Miss Laura. My first recollection of her was when she made fun of a jacket I had on. When I was a boy, I never liked anyone that made sport of me and if it was a boy there was sure to be a "mix-up" without regard as to who got "licked." If it was a girl, I just satisfied myself with hating her and her presence at any time would send me away sulking. My mother had bought a piece of broadcloth to make a wrap for one of my older sisters and afterwards found that it was not enough to make the cloak. I generally wore jeans of a sort of woolen cloth and when mother told me she intended to take the broadcloth that was not sufficient for my sister's garment and make me a roundabout, as that kind of garment was called in those days, I was almost too happy to sleep until it was done. When it was finished at last and I sauntered out with it, almost too proud to notice anyone, I encountered Miss Laura playing with my sister Anna and some others about our ages. Everyone complimented me on my nice new roundabout and I was feeling like a prince. The roundabout had a sort of point in the back that extended below the waistband. Miss Laura ran behind me and exclaimed "Why, Bob, the steeple on your jacket is upside down." I was fighting mad in a minute but as it was a girl that said it, I had to smother my wrath and say nothing. No man or boy at the time of my bringing up would dare to "sass back," as the negroes said, to a woman or girl. Soon after that, we moved away to the country and it was a long time before I met her; long after she had forgotten me and the jacket both. She was Mrs. Kaiser then and we both had a hearty laugh when I related the incident.

Mr. Hough was a very polished gentleman and always wore a black silk hat and a suit of clothes to correspond. His hat looked like it had just come out of the bandbox and he was noted for carrying a large silk handkerchief which he would frequently use for smoothing down his silk hat. They told a good joke on him after the wreck of the first train over the Missouri Pacific railroad to this place. The train went through the Gasconade bridge. A great many people were killed and injured by this accident. Mr. Hough, or Colonel as he was then called, was on the train. Someone saw him uninjured sitting on a log on the bank of the river and he had the famous handkerchief in his hand trying to smooth his silk hat which had come out of the wreck more battered than the owner. He would laugh about it when told him and say that a ruling passion would be strong even in death.

Mr. Hough was a fine speaker on public occasions. He delivered the first Fourth of July oration I ever heard and I remember how I thought that someday I would be called on to deliver a public oration and it would be the height of my ambition to deliver one just like Mr. Hough. I am now almost in the "sear and yellow leaf" and have not yet been called and as long as the people keep sane I never will be. I can't remember when I last heard an oration on the Fourth of July and yet before the war there never was a Fourth passed but somewhere in the town or county a speech was made on the natal day. In the past, someone read the Declaration of Independence on the

Fourth of July and the people gathered at picnics or barbecues to hear it. Good old days, good old people; they only live in our memories. But we are better that there were such people and such times.

R. E. Young

JEFFERSON INQUIRER PRINTING OFFICE

1845-1848
ANOTHER INTERESTING LETTER FROM DR. YOUNG

THE MISSOURI STATE TRIBUNE, SATURDAY EVENING MARCH 2, 1901
PAGE 1, COLUMNS 5-6

To the Editor of the State Tribune:
    Before reaching the Barcroft house on the corner of Main and Madison streets after leaving my home described in my last letter, you passed a deep gully now filled by what is known as Brown's Row on the right and a deep pond on the left now filled up and occupied by a vacant lot, Hendy's blacksmith shop, Moore's stable, and the Old Methodist church. I think Hendy's shop occupies what was about the middle of the pond. We boys often floated sailboats of a miniature type on the bosom of this pond in the summer and skated on it in the winter. I think it was the muddiest pond I ever saw and it seemed impossible to play on its banks without falling in to some extent - anyhow, you could manage it. When the weather was suitable, we frequently went down in the deep gully across the street from the pond and played making mud pies and rolling the mud into hard balls and throwing them from long willow switches at people or at windows but generally at each other till we wound up in a general war. One of the girls that played with us was Mary Gunn, who in after years graced the Governor's mansion as the wife of Gov. Gratz Brown. She was the first lady to occupy the present mansion and its magnificent proportions and adaptability in entertaining large crowds was largely due to her suggestions. She held the first reception within its walls and none since have filled it with more grace than she. The large painting of her husband was presented to her by friends and she received it through the eloquence of the late Major Rollins of Columbia and ordered its place over the mantel in the library. It was the initiatory of placing the portraits of ex-governors in the mansion.
    The Barcroft house was in later years the post office. Just between it and the old Episcopal Church on Madison street was the Reed Christy residence. It was a frame two-story house. Mr. Christy died in it during the cholera epidemic of 1851 and after the war, it together with the Barcroft house fell victims to fire. Where the

Madison House now stands were some one-story houses but I do not remember who lived in them. North on Madison are two houses of the olden times that still remain. One is occupied by Mrs. Dr. [C. A.] Thompson and the other by Mrs. Frazier. Opposite, or nearly so, was the old governor's mansion, a two-story brick with a one-story annex to the south used as the governor's office. The street had not been graded and the ground in front of these two houses now occupied by Mrs. Dr. Thompson [117 Madison] and Mrs. Frazier [115 Madison] was nearly as high as the two porticos in front of those buildings.

Again, I am thus precise in describing this locality for it was the playground to the school house which was in the building occupied by Mrs. Dr. Thompson. Mr. Calvin Gunn, editor of the *Jeffersonian*, occupied the house now the residence of Mrs. Frazier. The lower rooms of Mrs. [Maria] Thompson's house were used as a school house for boys and the upper floor of the school building for a girls' school. Both were private and taught independent of each other. The stairs leading to the girls' school went up from the rear. The boys played in front over the ground described above as far up the street as the Episcopal Church and as far down as the Basey[*] House, formerly described as the "Rising Sun Inn." The girls played on the lots now occupied by Reid's Laundry [201 E. Main] and Heinrichs' furniture establishment [207 E. Main].

The first teacher I ever went to at this place was Hon. Frank Hereford who afterwards was United States Senator from West Virginia. He was a splendid teacher and was one of the few that I knew as a teacher who was popular with both pupils and parents. He was a great whipper but whipped only for two things that I remember - idleness or fighting. You had to know your lesson when you went to recite or he would threaten you and the next time he whipped you. He whipped on the hand with a willow switch of which he kept a full supply locked up in his desk. For fighting, he whipped all concerned in the fight and would not listen to any explanations. The only way you could escape punishment for fighting was to not strike back and come and tell him. The boys of those days would rather fight any time and take the whipping from the teacher than to be laughed at by their play-fellows and called "tattle-tale."

---

[*] Basye

Once he caught a play-fellow and me in a fight just as he came to the school house. He called "books" and as soon as all were in their seats, he called Billy James and me before him. He asked us if any others were in the fight. Getting no reply, he said: "I saw you two," and proceeded to lick us, after which he proceeded with the school as if nothing had occurred.

Once there was a kind of general scrap in which nearly the whole school was engaged. Many of the larger boys hated to take their medicine and two rebelled. They ran out of the school house and went home. The parents of one of the boys made him return and when Mr. Hereford called him up, he showed fight. The teacher said: "No doubt you think I can't punish you but I can and will." There was a large tin-plate stove in the room and it was summertime. When Mr. Hereford had over-powered the young man, to add to his chagrin he placed him up and chucked his head into this stove. Us little fellows thought this was fine fun and hurrahed for the teacher. The other boy kept hanging about the playground and when "books" was called, would skulk away. One day, Mr. Hereford told him he must come to school or play somewhere else. At this, he threw a rock and hit the teacher and attempted to escape but the boys "nailed" him and brought him into the room and he had to take a double portion of what the teacher called a sound thrashing. After that time, he came right along to school but had several fights afterwards on account of the fun the boys poked at him.

I was not what was called a roll of honor scholar. My idea in those days was that the chief object of schools was to keep a boy from playing when he wanted to. I had lots of friends among the larger boys and not being industrious, would often get them [to] "do my sums" for me. Mr. Hereford soon caught on to this doing of mine and made me stand by him and do the work over after I had erased the work shown him as mine. Of course I failed and then the licking came.

It seems to me now, that on account of my directions in study and frequent fighting, I got licked about once a day on an average. Mr. Hereford told my father in a conversation about me, that he could never make me cry and he did not believe he could without being cruel. Father said: "I can make him yell like I was killing him but he won't cry [for] he thinks that is too much like a girl."

Good old school days of my early life! You will never return! I wanted to whip the teacher at the time and longed for the day when I would become a man and put in execution my thousand and one resolves in that direction. A sadness creeps over me often when in the wakeful hours of night I call up the dear old faces of Hereford's school. At this time, I remember Sam Owens, George Steele, Tenne Mathews, George Roots,[*] Ern Cordell, Adam Schwartzott, Bass McHenry, Nat Lynn, Nat Hough, Billy McCarty, John Basey[*] and a host of others. Some are living; the majority have passed "over" the river and are resting under the trees on the other side.   ***R. E. Young***

THE OLD EXECUTIVE OFFICE AND MANSION

---

[*] Rootes, Basye

HOW THE BOYS OF JEFFERSON CITY
AMUSED THEMSELVES YEARS AGO

THE MISSOURI STATE TRIBUNE, MONDAY MORNING MARCH 11, 1901
PAGE 2, COLUMNS 3-4

To the Editor of the State Tribune:

I am loath to leave the Hereford school for there are so many pleasant recollections connected with it. One of our chief plays in those days was the game called shinny. It was played with a ball and a stick crooked on the end something like the golf stick today. Two boys would choose for position and then they would choose thus about from the boys that would play until the whole school was chosen. A line was made up and down the middle of the street from Grace church south to the Basey[*] mansion north by means of some sharp iron instrument. About the middle of this line, the games began. The object was to get the ball "home" as it was called. One side's "home" was at Grace church south and the other side's "home" was at the Basey[*] mansion north. The stick was called a "shinny" and the rules of the game required you to play on your own side of the line. You were allowed to come over the line to hit the ball with your "shinny" stick but you must face your opponent and if you got faced the wrong way, your opponent could hit you lightly on your shins and say "shinny on your own side." If you refused to obey the injunction, he was allowed to hit you harder.

The game began, as I have said, in the middle of the line. The captains tossed the ball after deciding by a hand-over-hand measurement as to who should have the first strike after this fashion: "High buck or low doe." If the captain of the side which had the choice said "high buck" then the ball was tossed up and the game began at once by trying to hit the ball, both captains striking at it from opposite directions. If the choice was "low doe," the ball was dropped and both captains struck at the ball as before and the game began.

The hand-over-hand measurement was done by tossing up a stick and grabbing it as it came down. When caught by one captain, the other placed his hand over the one who caught the stick. Thus,

---

[*] Basye

they placed their hands alternately over each others until the end of the stick was reached. The one whose hand was at the end must have hold enough to toss the stick over his own head backwards. The one losing choice had to toss the ball while the winner had nothing to do but watch his opportunity to strike the ball. As soon as the ball struck the ground, the scramble began and the air was rent with the cry: "Shinny on your own side." When the teacher was not present, there was great danger of a "mix-up" as the boys say nowadays.

Sometimes ladies and gentlemen would get struck by the ball in passing up and down the street and complaints would be made but nothing seemed to be able to prevent the game. In the winter time, gentlemen played it on the ice. I remember once, they brought my father home on a stretcher, the result of falling on the ice while playing the game on skates. Once, when Governor Edwards was coming up Main street from the capitol, a small rock that one of the boys hit while striking at the ball hit the Governor in the breast. He went up to the boy and tapping him lightly on the head told him he ought to be more careful. The boy ran home and told his father and grown-up brother that the Governor struck him with his cane.

There was trouble at once for in those particular days, Governors were not thought to be made out of any better stuff than the ordinary mortal. When Governor Edwards found that he had mortally wounded the feeling of two of his townsmen, he sent for my father, a friend of his, and his own brother, Judge E. L. Edwards, to see the parties and tell them he had not intended to hurt or punish the boy but only to caution him to be more careful. The father of the boy, standing on his dignity, said: "The Governor will have to apologize with hat in hand." My father then "got on his ear," so to speak, and replied: "He will never do that and so far as the Governor is concerned that closes the matter." I relate this incident to show how independent and fearless were the people at that date. The incident was in a fair way to end in a duel but less hot-headed men than Judge Edwards and my father took hold of the matter and it was settled amicably and honorably to both parties. As much as this incident excited the people, it did not stop the game of "shinny" on our playground.

The playground at the school was not suited for playing "town ball" or "cat." In the long summer afternoons and on Saturdays, we played these games in what was known as "Locust Grove." This grove was about eight or ten feet above the present grade of High and Monroe streets. It extended to the alley between Main and High streets to High street and on the west to the Kentucky Saloon [221 E. High] and perhaps the ground now occupied by that saloon. The trees were principally along the street front, leaving a large area of ground free from trees. Here all the circuses were held and the ring they made lasted from one year to another.

This ring furnished the ground plan for "town ball," "cat," and "bull pen." There were three or four "bases" around the edge of the ring and the pitcher stood about the middle of the ring and pitched the ball to the man that stood on the middle base. There were two sides as in baseball - one at the bat and one in the field. There was also a catcher back of the striker and he, like the pitcher, belonged to the same side. When the ball was struck or struck at three times, the batter had to make the first base before he was hit with the ball or he was out. He was also out if anyone caught the ball while flying or if it had only hit the ground one time or as they said "caught on the first bounce," or if the ball thrown by a fielder passed between him and the base he was trying to make. When all the batters were put out, then the fielders took the bat and that was called one game. This game was "town ball."

"Bull pen" was played by choosing up sides as in the other games. The ones having the choice took the ball and the others went in a ring formed by four or five "bases" placed in a circle. The ball was pitched across the ring to the ones on the "bases." After pitching the ball two or three times across the ring, some pitcher would throw the ball at those in the pen and those on the "bases" would run away. If the pitcher failed to hit anyone and that one or someone of his side did not hit one of the men on the "bases," then he was out. When they got down to one or two on a side, the game was very exciting.

I went to several schools taught at the Hereford school house as described before. I think Dr. Duncan Lynn taught after Mr. Hereford quit to study law. He was popular with the patrons but not with the boys like Hereford. I do not remember any distinguishing features connected with his school. I think he taught between medical lectures. I never went but one time to him. I remember him more as a young doctor than as a teacher. He died early in life in Maries county while practicing his profession.

One of the early characters of Jefferson City taught the last school I attended at the Hereford house.   He was called Prof. Bingham.   He was about six feet and two inches in height, raw-boned or angular in build, and red-headed.   When he got mad, he was a holy terror.   He whipped and whipped hard the boys said [but] he never licked me.   All he had to do at any time to settle me was to draw his shaggy-red eyebrows down and look straight at me and I was as meek as Moses.

There were two boys who came to his school named Ainsworth - Bob and Bill.   Their father was a stonecutter and a stonemason.   He was, like my father, much away from home contracting.   For some offense against the teacher's rules, Prof. Bingham sought to correct Billy Ainsworth by whipping.   Billy wouldn't stand the punishment and ran off from school.   A few days after, the Professor saw Billy across the street playing.   He left the school room and collared Billy and brought him into the school room and whipped him to his heart's content.   At noon recess, Billy went home and soon after "books" had been called in the afternoon, Mrs. Ainsworth came rushing into the school room as "terrible as an army with banners" and proceeded at once to business by grabbing the stove lid off the stove and throwing it at the Professor's head.   He was a good dodger and she missed him.   Before she could get the poker which would have been a deadly weapon in her hands, the Professor caught her and was holding her at arm's length when Dr. A. M. Davison who was passing and heard the noise, ran in and commanded the Professor to let go of the woman.   But he was in a situation of the fellow who attacked the wild cat - he needed someone to help him let go.   He called on Dr. Davison to hold the woman [for] he didn't need anyone to hold him.   By this time, we children were out of the school house ready to take to our heels.   Some more men came in and it took them all to pacify Mrs. Ainsworth who was removed from the room and the Professor was left in peaceful possession of the room.   He called us in and told us he would give us the rest of the day off.

R. E. Young

RETROSPECTIVE
DR. YOUNG'S REMINISCENCES OF THE DAYS LONG AGO.
INTERESTING ANECDOTES AND SKETCHES OF JEFFERSON CITY'S CITIZENS OF ANTEBELLUM DAYS

THE MISSOURI STATE TRIBUNE, MONDAY MORNING MARCH 18, 1901
PAGE 8, COLUMNS 1-6

To the Editor of the State Tribune:

Just across the street from the Hereford school house, as before described, stood the old executive office and mansion. At the time of which I write, it was occupied by Governor John C. Edwards. Gov. Edwards was an emigrant from East Tennessee to Missouri. He had an imposing personality; was more than six feet in height and slightly embonpoint. His was a kindly face and his manners were rather reserved although he was an approachable man. He was a bachelor at the time he was Governor and I remember him as extremely fond of children. He used to visit our house quite often as he was fond of my father. He frequently played with us children and seemed to enter into our childish sports with great zest. Once, he knocked at our door when father and mother were not at home. My eldest sister [Mary] opened the door and when she saw who it was, she called back to my youngest sister, Ann, and me who were making too much noise to be still as it was Governor Edwards. Sister Ann said: "Who cares for the governor!" She was about seven years old. The governor heard her and was so pleased with her independence of character that he sent her a present of a rocking chair which is in the family yet.

Governor Edwards had been in politics prominently as State senator before he was governor. In the winter season, he wore a cloak something like the one that appears in the picture of Col. [Thomas Hart] Benton now hanging in the capitol. In general appearance, he was not unlike Benton although he was in politics an anti-Benton Democrat. He made a successful and popular Governor and if he had not caught the gold fever of 1849 and emigrated to California, he would doubtless have reached the United States Senate. I think he obtained some prominence in the politics of California but was greatly handicapped by being a Democrat.

Next to the Hereford school house was the residence of Calvin Gunn. He was a printer and at the time of which I write, published a weekly paper. I think it was called the *Jeffersonian* and was edited by Judge E. L. Edwards, brother of the Governor. Mr. Gunn had a large family and until he was paralyzed in 1850, he was well to do in the world. His trouble was supposed to have been brought on by the use of leaden type in the printing business. Sometimes, before Mr. Gunn was confined to his bed by a stroke of paralysis, he would imbibe a little too much of John Barley Corn. At such times, he would walk up and down the street in his shirt sleeves with his thumbs under his suspenders and his hand directed to the front and upwards. At such times - and they were not frequent - he would stop everyone he met and it was difficult to get away from him. He remembered all the children and had some joke to tell on most of them.

He had a son named after him who, at the time about which I am writing, was one of my big boy friends. His name was Calvin after his father and he was about six or seven years my senior. Cal was fond of hunting, had a gun, and kept dogs. He was the only boy my mother would let me go a hunting with and he always liked to have me go because I thought Cal was the *ne plus ultra* in everything connected with hunting. I would obey him more implicitly than I would even my father and mother because he once in a while allowed me to shoot. I "turned" the squirrels for him and picked up the game he killed and carried the most of it. He was fair and always divided with me. And when in 1849 he ran away from home and went to California in search of gold, I lost a friend out of my young life that was never replaced.

It seemed to me that nearly all of my big boy friends went to California. Two of them I will mention here, Billy Wells and George Steele. Billy Wells was a son of Judge Wells of whom I have before spoken. We were friends because, and there is always a because for friendships, he had a pony and would let me ride him to water and climb up in the hay loft and throw down the hay sometimes. When he wanted to play marbles with some of the big boys, he would let me hold the pony. And when he was in a right good humor, he would let me ride him to the stable and pat him. Sometimes I rode him further than the stable but I was careful to get back and put him up before Billy found it out. After Billy ran away and went to California, there was no more pony riding for me.

George Steele was my big boy friend because he would stop his work any time to help me out of the intricacies of arithmetic. George never seemed to study much and still he always knew his lessons. He was the best player of any game to be played at the school and when he was not one of the captains, he was always the first choice of which side had the first choice. I don't remember ever to have seen him in a fight of his own but in almost every fight he seemed to be the chosen umpire as it were to see that both sides had fair play.

I remember once he caused me a whipping while we were going to the Hereford school. We sat behind long slanting desks and George sat next to me. He had bored a hole in the top of the desk with his knife and several smaller ones leading into it from different directions. All these holes he had plugged with wooden pins. He caught flies and put them in the largest hole and when it was full, he would draw a pin from one of the smaller holes and let the fly that might appear escape. I saw him pull one of the small pins out and a fly escaped. George made out as though he would catch the fly and that made me laugh "out loud" as we used to say. Hereford called me up and wanted to know what I was laughing at. I looked at George and the expression of his eye seemed to say: "I'll lick you if you tell." I was between two fires. If I didn't tell, Hereford would lick me for disturbing the school. If I did tell, George might lick me for telling and besides, if he didn't, I was sure to get the displeasure of my fellows and be called a "tattle tale." I couldn't afford that, for I had made a reputation for never telling. And so I said I didn't know what made me laugh and took Hereford's licking and added another feather to my cap as one who would not tell.

Next to the Gunn residence was the Basey[*] House. As I remember Major Basey,[*] he was about 6 feet tall and as erect as an Indian. He was a large man for his height and had a pleasant face. I do not remember much about him but am inclined to think from this great distance of time since I knew him that he was fond of his ease and personal comfort. My recollection is that he was kind and gentle in his manners. I also remember that he was popular and well liked by his neighbors.

In one of my former letters, I made him the innkeeper in a story told to me by those who were there then. Since then I have learned

---

[*] Basye

that I made mistakes in that letter and that the name was John Smith T. and not John Smith R. as I had it. John C. Gordon was the host of the inn and not Major Basey* as I thought. My only excuse for these errors is that the incident was told to me later. It happened before I was born.**

Major Basey* had a large family at the time of which I write. I only knew one of them, John. He was much older than me, perhaps six or seven years. He went to the Hereford school and was an associate of Sam Owens, Billy Wells, Cal Gunn, George Steele and boys of that age. I do not remember much of him at the time but in later years I knew him as one of the fashionably dressed men about town. They used to tell a story on him that will do to repeat here. They said he went with the engineering crew to locate the line of the Missouri railway beyond here. On the day they were to start, John showed up in a buggy with a negro to drive and had on kid gloves. They asked him where he was going and when they told him he would have to walk, he declined to go.

Major Basey* had another son which I knew in after years but did not know him when we lived in town. Dr. Alfred Basey* was one of many of God's noblemen. He died in the Confederate army and was my friend. I revere his memory.

R. E. Young

---

* Basye
** Gordon started the Rising Sun in 1826 and by 1840 Major Basye was the innkeeper.

HOW PEOPLE USED TO GO TO CHURCH
IN JEFFERSON CITY

THE MISSOURI STATE TRIBUNE, SATURDAY EVENING MARCH 23, 1901
PAGE 1, COLUMNS 5-6

To the Editor of the State Tribune:

The place where the Madison House now stands in 1849 was occupied by two or three one-story frame buildings and the street in front of them was much higher than at present. I think there would have been no steps necessary to get into the Madison House if the street had not been graded down from its natural heights. The first house above these houses towards High street was the brick building now occupied by a restaurant and adjoining Mr. Wm. Ross' residence.

This building, at the time about which I am writing, was occupied by a saloon. This is somewhat a historic building. "Uncle" Howard Barnes for nearly a generation kept a restaurant there. "Uncle" Howard must be nearly 90 years old. He was a slave in 1849 and went with his master to California where he obtained his freedom when that state was admitted into the Union.

But long before "Uncle" Howard had a restaurant there, the building had a history. During the Harrison campaign of 1840 someone kept a saloon there. Politics ran high in the first Harrison campaign and this town was nearly equally divided on the issues of the day with a slight Democratic majority. A certain steamboat plied the Missouri River in those days and her captain was a strong Benton adherent. He had the hurricane roof of his boat decked with a log cabin, the symbol of the Whigs' campaign. In one of the heated arguments at the old Hervidian Hotel, the stone house on Water street previously described, the Democrats threatened when his boat returned down the river that if he had that log cabin on the roof of the boat, they would hoist a pole with a red petticoat on it for a flag.

The Democrats claimed that in some of the battles against the Indians up in the Lake region, Gen. Harrison had showed the white feather and one of their counter moves against the log cabin exhibited was a red petticoat indicating that he ought to be a woman and protected against the requirement of the country to bear arms. In a short time after the argument at the hotel, the boat returned with the log cabin aboard. The pole was ready and when the boat was in sight, the Democrats hoisted it with the red petticoat on top. The boat did not land and then the Democrats began twitting the Whigs.

The storm grew more fierce as time wore on and on a certain day the Whigs assembled at this saloon above described and threatened to wade through Democratic blood up to the armpits. The Democrats had assembled at a saloon somewhere near where the Schott saloon now is and after imbibing considerably, started for the saloon where the Whigs were. About where the Handly grocery store now is, they met a friendly colored man and he told them: "For God's sake do not go down dar for dem Whigs are going to wade in your blood up to de armpits." But they went on and in front of the saloon a parley was held when a non-combatant, as it were, named Bartlett came out of the saloon and advised them not to enter. By this time calmer and wiser councils prevailed on both sides, and the Democrats and Whigs put down arms and took a drink all around.

At another time, a fight occurred in this saloon at which time a man by the name Greene was killed by John Perry. Perry's father lived some six or seven miles west of town and was well-known. It about broke the old gentleman up to clear John but he managed to do it.

Just in rear of the Madison House on Main street stands the old Presbyterian Church. At the time of which I write, it was one of the principal places of worship in the town. Here my family worshipped and here we children attended Sunday-school. Often, when I pass it, fond and sad memories come rushing in my imagination. I can see the dear old people sitting in their pews. There on the front seat in the center row of pews sits P. T. Miller and Henry Cordell. They are deacons and pass the basket for collection. But their chief business is to teach and manage the Sunday-school and raise the tune when the minister gives out the hymn; he says long meter, short meter, and difficult meter. It was all Greek to me but they understood their business and the people follow them as best they can - some a little too fast, others a little too slow, some off a higher key than the leader's pitch and still others a little lower than proper. But all sing. Everybody sings and the Lord accepts it as honorable to satiate in truth.

There on the extreme right, as you go in, sits Brother Lamb and his family, devout Scotch Presbyterians. Brother Lamb is a stonecutter and does honest and true work all the week. He remembers the Sabbath day to keep it holy. He cuts his wood on Saturday and piles it up for Sunday when he will do the least amount of labor in using it. His "gude" wife prepares the food on Saturday and there are no Sunday dinners at Sister Lamb's.

On the same side but in the center row of pews sits Brother McHenry and his family. The children have been to Sunday School and now sit with their parents during services. Brother McHenry is a carpenter and no man ever accused him of slighting his work. He is a good man and content with his lot in life. He once told my father: "I would not go out contracting and live away from my family like you do for all the money in the world."

I imagine I can see E. B. Cordell and his family sitting in the center row of pews about the middle of the church. He was the merchant prince of the town at that time. He comes in a little late. His wife and children have preceded him. He is a good, honest dealer and loved by all the people. His children sit with him in the family pew.

On the right hand side on the front side pew sits Dr. [William] Bolton and his family. They live three miles from town at the place known now as the Berry farm. They have come to church in a closed carriage with a colored driver on the seat outside. The Doctor has ridden in behind the carriage (old Virginia and North Carolina style). The Doctor leads the way up the aisle and stands at the entrance of the pew until his wife enters and arranges the children. Then he takes his seat at the outer end of the pew. He is a fine specimen of the southern gentleman - polite to point of punctiliousness. But the character in this family is Sister [Sarah Landsdown] Bolton. She is dressed to the point of the existing fashions. Her children are neat and clean and dressed in good style. She places each one in the pew exactly as she wants them to sit, smoothes down whatever wrinkles are in their clothes by reason of the riding three miles in the carriage, and then she sits down herself and appears to say mentally everything is "goriak," a word she frequently used in conversation when things suited her exactly. There they sit - Josephine, Cecelia, Ophelia and Theodosia[*] - as good-looking and well-behaved a family as the most zealous Presbyterians could wish.

On the side aisle to the left near the center of the church sits Wm. Penninger and his family. They, too, have come to church a distance of five miles. They have come in a spring wagon or maybe horseback. Brother and Sister Penninger are sturdy Presbyterians. They have emigrated to Missouri from the state of Maryland. Brother Penninger has a large family and they are all with him at church.

I see P. T. Miller and his family in my imagination. They consist of himself and wife and George and Louisa. There are other children but they are too small to attend church. He sits, as I have said before, on the front center pew with Henry Cordell to do the leading in singing. The family sits in the next pew behind him. Henry Cordell's family sit in the same pew to the right. (The center tier of pews have no division in them but extend from aisle to aisle.) Mrs. Cordell with her sons Tom, Dick, and Harry are in this pew.

In the next directly behind Henry Cordell's family sits Wm. C. Young, wife, and four children. Brother Young sits next to the aisle. Then come the children - Robert, Mary, Josephine, and Ann. Brother Young sits straight up in the pew as though he was lashed to a pole and looks straight at the preacher. He now and then takes a side glance at "Bob" to see if he is asleep. The mother looks after the girls and Ann sits next to her. Bob would give anything he had on earth to swap seats with Ann. He is the youngest and only boy and it would be hard to keep Mother from allowing him to nestle up to her and take a nap while the preacher was deep in some theological subject. But the strict Presbyterian father has anticipated this and makes Bob sit next to him with the three girls between him and the mother.

Where are the negroes of all these godly people? As many of them as choose to be are in the pews next to the door or at some other church of their choice.

R. E. Young

---

[*] Dr. Young may have confused this name. According to James F. McHenry, a Bolton Family descendant, their were eleven children, none of which was named Theodosia. The other names are correct. The full names of those mentioned are: Josephine Bonaparte Bolton, Mary Cecelia Bolton, and Ophelia Lewis Bolton.

CHANGES THAT HAVE OCCURRED
IN JEFFERSON CITY

THE MISSOURI STATE TRIBUNE, SATURDAY EVENING MARCH 30, 1901
PAGE 1, COLUMNS 5-6

To the Editor of the State Tribune:

I cannot and ought not to quit the old Presbyterian church of Jefferson City without describing its beloved pastor. The Rev. John G. Fackler was a tall but well-built man, graceful in carriage, and rather quick in movement. He had black hair and wore a short beard without mustache and had the German's [illegible]. His voice was deep and musical, his enunciation clear and distinct, his gesticulations gave force and effect to his utterances and taken as together, he was a pleasant speaker. His eyes had a kindly light in them that never failed to interest children. He was the children's friend. Everybody in the church liked him and when he was called away to St. Joseph to a wider field, the people felt they would never look upon his like again.

He had quit a thriving mercantile business to enter upon the ministry and if anyone was ever called of God to preach the Gospel, he surely was. He was like the Presbyterian preachers of those days and could pray a prayer so long that to my boy mind appeared to include the whole human family now living and that might in the future ages live. His sermons were written and father said they were argumentative and exhaustive. All I know is that they exhausted me and by the time the benediction was offered, the prospect of a cold dinner was as alluring to me as any repast ever furnished by Tony Faust or Delmonico for that matter.

What makes Presbyterian and Methodist preachers pray so long? Well, I guess that question will never be answered. If the long prayers are required, the small boy who had his prayer type written and posted up on the wall back of the bed will have a poor shock, for he only pointed at the written prayer and exclaimed: "Lord these are my sentiments," and jumped into bed. I suppose there is a happy medium in prayer as in everything else.

The Presbyterians were very set in their ways as was demonstrated a few years later than the time of which I am writing. My sister Josephine, Miss Bettie Roots,[*] and Miss Bettie Miller conceived the idea of having an organ in the church. They succeeded in accomplishing the undertaking but it divided the people and came near breaking up the congregation. My! wouldn't they turn over in their graves if they knew the church was desecrated by the sound of a cornet, horn, or fiddler. Who knows? The people now on earth may live to see the "dancing before the Lord" as in the olden time. The world goes round and round and "there is nothing new under the sun."

A little below the church and on the other side of Main street about where Clark's Row begins was a two-story frame house occupied by Peter McClain. What Mr. McClain followed I do not remember if I ever knew. I only remember that a man by that name lived there. Just on the corner where Ott's lumber yard [site of the Jefferson State Office Building] now is was a two-story frame house with the stairs to the upper story going up on the outside to a porch that extended the full length of the front. Whoever lived here I never knew.

Just east of the house was a long, deep pond made by the filling of the street at this point. On the other side of Jefferson street and on the corner of Main and Jefferson streets was a two-story brick house painted white and known in its early days as the "white house." In this house, on the 29th day of February, the author of these letters was born. According to Alzira McCarty there was raging at the time the biggest snowstorm that ever struck Jefferson City. The house stood on the ground now occupied by the modern residence of Louis Ott [site of the Missouri Department of Transportation Headquarters]. Some years ago it was torn down and rebuilt on High street by the late Pete Miller. Not far from this house on the opposite side of Main street was the old market house. It was built large enough for a market house suited to the present age of Jefferson City. It was never occupied as a market house in the time of which I am writing. If it was I did not know.

Main street in those days extended through where the capitol grounds now are and there was a pond somewhere near the present site of the supreme court building caused by a fill in the street at this point. There was a deep gully opposite this pond that extended to the river, and across this gully was a flat log about three feet in width. This log

---

[*] Rootes

became famous by Dr. Lynn riding a spirited horse across the gully on it. Somewhere in this region back of Mrs. Rogers' house was the spring that supplied this portion of the town with water. It was walled up with stone, and had a stone covering over it.

Once when I was going on some errand in this locality, I spied two little girls down in this deep gully. They had been playing in the gully and now found themselves unable to get out. My recollection is that they were crying. When they saw me, they called to me to come and help them out. When I got down there, I found the young misses to be Celeste Price and her cousin Amanda Wells. They were a sight to behold - almost covered with mud. I helped them out and placed them on terra firma. Then for the first time in my young life, I experienced that all girls were not nuisances and that a boy could wait on some one of them and run errands for her with delight instead of trouble. From that time, when we play "King William" and "post office" and other childish games, I was glad when Celeste Price chose me and mad when she chose some other boy.

For the sake of some of my young friends, I will explain the games of "King William" and "post office." In "King William," the boys and girls joined hands and moved around a circle in the center of which a boy or a girl stood as the case might require. They all sang the following words to a pleasing tune and at the proper time, the one in the center tried to catch someone in the circle - everyone trying to keep from being caught. The words were as follows:

> *King William was King James' son,*
> *And from the royal race he sprung,*
> *Go choose your east, go choose your west,*
> *Go choose the one that you love best,*
> *If she's not here to take your part,*
> *Go choose another with all your heart.*

Then the race began. After one had been caught by the one in the center, the circle formed again and moved around the couple in the center singing:

> *Down on the carpet you must kneel,*
> *As sure as the grass grows in the field,*
> *Salute your bride with kiss so sweet,*
> *Now you may rise upon your feet.*

Then the last one chosen - boy or girl - would remain in the center and the game would proceed as before.

Two rooms or a room and a hall were required for playing "post office." They would choose by drawing straws or in some other way who should go out in the hall. The one in the hall would open the door and exclaim that there was a letter in the post office for someone, naming the person. The one named would have to go out in the hall and then there was a race and scramble for the letter which was a kiss. The one who went for the letter remained in the hall and announced who the next letter was for and so the game continued until the children were tired or had to go home.

These games were only played by the children and youths. The young ladies and gentlemen danced as they do now. Miss Celeste Price was the daughter of Gen. Thos. L. Price. Miss Amanda Wells was her first cousin and now the Widow Dunlap[*] of Centretown. Miss Celeste Price became the wife of Col. Celsus Price, my roommate and classmate at college and my comrade in the rebel army. She was a beautiful and lovely girl and devoted wife. She had many suitors and although her father was a Union General, she married her rebel lover. She fell a victim of cholera that swept over St. Louis in 1866.

R. E. Young

---

[*] Mrs. A. W. Dunlap

A BIT OF HISTORY
CONCERNING A CONTRACT BETWEEN THE STATE AND JEFFERSON CITY

THE MISSOURI STATE TRIBUNE, FRIDAY[*] EVENING APRIL 6, 1901
PAGE 4, COLUMNS 5-6

To the Editor of the State Tribune:
    That part of Main street within the capitol inclosure was a steep ascent to a point opposite the south door of the capitol building then a rapid descent until you reached the eastern approach to the Ware's creek bridge. To give you some idea of how high the hill was, you must consider that the basement windows now to be seen above ground were at that time under ground and had areas with grating over the top. When Governor [Robert M.] Stewart purchased the ground south of Main street, the city vacated that part of Main street passing through the capitol enclosure and for this gift, the State agreed to keep in good repair that portion of Main street from the eastern gate of the capitol grounds to the penitentiary lot. Gratz Brown was the only Governor that ever tried to observe this contract. He graded the street as it now exists with convict labor and the city macadamized it. The city has never been able to convince any other Governor that it was the duty of the State to keep Main street in repair.
    There were several houses along the east side of Washington street inside the present capitol grounds. On this site was a livery stable owned by a man by the name of Anderson. I do not remember him but knew his sons, Frank and Tham. Frank was a cripple and had to use a crutch but was one of the best marble players that attended Hereford's school. Frank was several years my senior and Tham three or four years my junior. Tham's mother used to visit our mother and bring Tham along. Mother made me stay at home on such occasions and entertain Tham. I thought he was too young for me to play with and of course, I voted him a bore. He was a good boy and I thought he would "tell" but he never did that I remember.
    Somewhere in this neighborhood lived one of the characters of Jefferson City in those days - Major Sandford. He was either a retired

---

[*] Misprinted Friday instead of Saturday

army officer or one that had resigned. He was fond of playing whist and other games at cards. In his general demeanor he was a quiet gentleman but sometimes he would get a little too much of the "critter" and then he was noisy and profane. He had a boon companion in the person of Judge Morrow who lived somewhere near the house now occupied by Sam Sone just west of the city limits. They would frequently get to drinking and raise considerable disturbance and Dangerfield Meredith, the city marshal, would have to correct them and threaten to lock them up. This threat generally quieted them and they either went home or some of their friends got them out of the way. Meredith never had the slightest idea of punishing them. Once they had been on a protracted spree and Meredith had made them angry by threatening them with the lock-up. Finally, they got "located," as the negroes used to say, on a goods box near Thalheimer's store and something like this conversation took place: "Major," said Morrow, "let's burn the town down; it is not fit for a gentleman to live in anyway."

The Major agreed to the plan and it was discussed between them how it should be done and when they would begin. But before they began, it was thought best and they were perfectly agreed upon the proposition that they had better take another drink. On coming out of the saloon after they had taken several drinks and discussed again and again the modus operandi, the Major said to the Judge: "Morrow, I agree perfectly with you and am decidedly in favor of the conflagration but, by gad, we will have to remove the women and children to a place of safety before we begin." His soldierly instincts were still sober.

There was another prominent character that lived in Major Sandford's neighborhood - Col. [James] Dunica.[*] He was noted for never giving a positive answer to any question that might be asked him. One day in March, he was seen coming down High street and nearing the Obermayer corner where General Thos. L. Price and some other gentlemen were talking. Price offered to bet Maryweather Jefferson the drinks for the crowd that he couldn't get a positive answer to any question he proposed to Dunica.[*] Jefferson took the bet and by that time Dunica[*] arrived. After shaking hands all around, Jefferson said: "Mr. Dunica,[*] this is a very blustery day, isn't it?" It

---

[*] Dunnica

was a March day and the wind was blowing almost a gale. Dunica[*] looked up at the sky and said: "Well, if it keeps on blowing it will be." Price called the boys to the Paulsel House and set 'em up.

South of the capitol on Main street was the residence of Mr. [James Bennett] McHenry, the father of our townsman Mr. James McHenry. He had a son about my age named Bass. We were fond of each other and were nearly always together on Saturdays. We were both in the rebel army and I believe he now lives in Memphis, Tenn. Then Bass was one of those fat kind and was generally in a good humor. He could climb any kind of tree and swim the Missouri River if necessary. James McHenry belonged to the older set and George belonged to a younger set than Bass and I. Mr. McHenry was so attached to his home that when they wanted him to sell his house and lot because it was in the addition to the capitol grounds, he would only consent to do so provided the state would build him one just like it on the south side of Stewart street just opposite.

I have spoken of Mr. Mathews in these letters before but it will bear repeating that Jefferson City never possessed a better citizen and the Presbyterian church not a more faithful or more consistent Christian within its folds.

After leaving the capitol grounds and continuing westward on Main street, there were no more houses until after you crossed the bridge over Ware's creek. Just beyond the bridge on the north side of the street where the gas works now are, was the "Inn By T. Mills: Refreshments for Man and Beast." Mr. Mills was a humble citizen and so far as I know kept a good tavern. Nearly all the country people coming from the western part of the county stopped with Thos. Mills. Not far from the Mills Inn there was a family by the name of [illegible] Beyond them to the west in a brick house lived the widowed sister of Jefferson T. Rodgers.[*] I am not now able to call her name.

After leaving this house, there were no others until you were near the top of Richmond Hill. There on the south side of Main street at the junction at Bolivar lived John B. Walters, grandfather of Dr. J. P. Porth, our present Representative. Mr. Walters kept a store of general merchandise. The country people living west of town nearly all dealt with him. It was a very handy store for the people had a sort of last chance there if they had forgotten to purchase up in the city.

---

[*] Dunnica, Rogers

"Uncle John," as nearly everyone called him, was a very obliging gentleman and had the reputation of selling cheap and dealing fairly.

Beyond the Walters store and on the right hand side of the street going westward was the residence of Mr. Lamb, a stonecutter and Scotchman. I have mentioned him before in these letters. He had a fine reputation for being strict and no doubt deserved it. We Presbyterian boys kept as clear of Mr. Lamb as much as possible, especially if we were being mischief. I don't know that he ever informed on us but we were afraid he would. He was fond of singing Scotch songs such as "Auld Lang Syne" and "Highland Laddy" and many a time I have stopped at his shop to hear him sing.

The last house on Main street was the Fulkerson residence. It was about opposite the present water tower. Fulkerson was a lame man and had a large family but they were younger. I knew some of them but they were too little in those days for me to remember them.

R. E. Young

THE
STATE CAPITOL
OF 1840

POLITICS AT THE STATE CAPITAL
FIFTY YEARS AGO

THE MISSOURI STATE TRIBUNE, SATURDAY EVENING APRIL 13, 1901
PAGE 1, COLUMNS 1-2

To the Editor of the State Tribune:

Beginning where High street touches Ware's creek and going east, the first house I remember was one on the corner of High and Broadway known as the Ferguson House. It was kept, at the time of which I write, by Wm. Ferguson. He had been in the Mexican War and was crippled in one hand and arm. He was a member of Capt. M. M. Parsons' company from Cole county. He kept a most excellent boarding house and was popular with the traveling and sojourning people. His good wife was a member of the Methodist Church, South and a very devout Christian. She could always be found at church on Sunday, at mid-week prayer meeting, and at every love feast.

The love feast was a common adjunct to the Methodist Church in those days and the good people frequently got so happy at them that they shouted. Mrs. Ferguson was frequently among the number that shouted. I wonder what the people would think now if some good sister would get so happy that she would shout. I suspect she would be called excited and weak in mental make-up. Religion is largely emotional, that is, it has to do with the emotions. The Christian religion is founded on the love of God and man. Love is emotional and not governed by reason. No man or woman ever loved logically and never will. Love may be accompanied with reason but oftener it is not. To be born again is to love God and the new birth is realized through the emotional nature and not by reason. Man cannot by reason enter into the new life but by obedience he can attain unto the love of God and thus become a new creature. But enough, someone may say I am preaching and I had better not for there is great danger I may not keep orthodox. I believe that if anyone feels like shouting, they ought to be allowed to shout.

THE FERGUSON HOUSE

The next house after leaving the Ferguson House was that of Gen. Thomas L. Price. The house has been enlarged in later years but retains the original plan. Gen. Price was the richest man in Jefferson City in the years of which I write and remained in that class till his death in 1870. He owned many slaves and had immigrated to this state from either Virginia or North Carolina. Coming to Missouri in the early thirties with slaves and capital, he found many opportunities to accumulate money. He was a close dealer and husbanded his resources and a man of great energy and industry. He was a fine-looking man in personal appearance and suave in manner.

He was popular and soon took an active part in politics and was a Democrat. Being an admirer of Col. Benton, he stood by the Senator when he disobeyed the instructions of the legislature and appealed to the people. Gen. Price became one of the leaders of the Benton party in Missouri and in fighting Benton's battles, he became estranged from many of his former Democratic friends who had arranged themselves against Col. Benton and became what was known as the anti-Benton Democracy. The Democratic party in Missouri was more fiercely separated in those days as Benton and anti-Bentonites than the gold-bug and silver-bug Democrats in recent years. They never did come together again but fought each other until 1860 when the Benton men became Union men and many of them merged into the Republican party while most of the anti-Benton party became rebels or rebel sympathizers. Gen. Price was loath to forgive the anti-Benton Democrats for voting with the Whigs and voting Guire* United States Senator to succeed Benton.

When the war came, it found Gen. Price a strong advocate of the Union. He had been elected to the legislature on what was known as the "freeman ticket" beating John Enloe, the candidate of the Breckenridge Democracy. When Clabe [Claiborne] Jackson essayed to take Missouri out of the Union, Gen. Price fought desperately against him. He was, for a time, in command of the military post established here and was always the friend of the old citizens who had been his former companions in the Democratic party before Benton fell. His character is formally illustrated in an incident that occurred early in the war and marked him as one of God's noblemen.

Many citizens of rebel sympathy had been arrested and put in prison as "Knights of the Golden Circle." Among the number was Gen. G. A. Parsons and my father, neither of whom had spoken to Price for fifteen years or more and both had had personal difficulties with him. A certain party then living in Jefferson City gave out that he had found the roster of the "Knights of the Golden Circle" and in proof of his assertion exhibited a paper with the names of many of the best citizens on it. The Federal officer then in command of the post had all these men arrested and thrown into prison. When Gen. Thomas L. Price heard of it (he was away at the time), he hastened home and demanded to see the list. When it was shown him he said: "I have known these gentlemen for many years and I know they would not be guilty of anything dishonorable. If they had intended to oppose the government, they would have gone south with their friends." He continued: "I know by his 'ear marks' the fellow that claims to have captured this so-called roster of the 'Knights of the Golden Circle.' This is a production of his fertile and dishonest brain."

---

* Henry S. Geyer

THOMAS LAWSON PRICE

Gen. Price continued his efforts as a loyal citizen with the Federal officer until these men were released from prison. As they were released, they went to him and thanked him for his efforts in their behalf and felt doubly thankful because he had acted without any solicitation on their part. Ever after they lived in peace and although he died before many of them, they remained his steadfast friends to the end.

After the war, Gen. Thomas L. Price came back into the Democratic party with Frank Blair and others like him and did Trojan work towards healing the wounds left by the great fratricidal war. Price died in the closing years of the disfranchisement mourned by the thousands he had tried to protect and restore to citizenship. He was a man of great courage and displayed it in several personal difficulties before the war. Once when Benton and anti-Benton was the war cry in Missouri politics, he was attacked in front of E. B. Cordell's store, now occupied by Weiser & Artz [201 E. High], by an anti-Benton Democrat named Hickman. Price was unarmed and Hickman had a revolver which was then just coming into use and displacing the deadly Derringer. Hickman made the assault and advanced on Price firing his six-shooter. Price rushed on him, took his revolver from him then thrashed him to his satisfaction. Price was wounded in three places. Hickman hit him every time he fired but did no great damage as the shots were glancing.

Before Gen. Price's death, he began building a college in the western part of the city which he intended to endow. But death overtook him when the building was only one story high and it was never completed. If he had lived, the home where his struggles of early manhood were made would have had a successful institution of learning for he was the kind of man that always succeeded. He died worth a half million dollars at an age when he had not much more than passed the meridian of life. He was a kind and indulgent master to his slaves. One, whom I had as janitor long after he was free, used to entertain me with stories of his master's kindness and indulgence. Gen. Price had three children by his first wife, who was a Miss Bolton. The oldest one was Napolean, a very bright boy and about my age. He died quite young and my father used to say the General never quite became reconciled to his death. His daughter was named Celeste, a beautiful girl of whom I have spoken in these letters and the

PRICE MANSION

PRESENT SITE OF THE
SUPREME COURT BUILDING

youngest son was named Thomas after his father. General Price made a large portion of his wealth in contracting on the Missouri Pacific railroad when it was being constructed.

R. E. Young

GHOST STORY
HOW BURR MCCARTY MADE BLACK HAWK SHOW SPEED

THE MISSOURI STATE TRIBUNE, SATURDAY EVENING APRIL 20, 1901
PAGE 1, COLUMNS 1-2

To the Editor of the State Tribune:

East from the Price mansion on the northeast corner of High and Washington streets was a two-story frame house. Jno. Frazer* had a school there at one time and I attended it. John Frazer* was a brother of our fellow townsman Henry Frazer* and uncle of Jim Frazer* the High street barber. He was a good and kind teacher and was popular with pupil and patron. Just how long he taught I do not remember. He was one of the first to study and practice taking pictures by the Daguerrean system in Jefferson City. We have pictures of all our family taken by him in 1850. His family was one of the first white families to locate in Jefferson City and his brother, Henry, now an old man, was the first white child born in the place.

The next house was on the north side of High street and was occupied by Henry Burger, the first merchant tailor in the place. He made my first tailor made coat and it wore until it was too small for me and a negro boy younger than me fell heir to it. Mr. Burger stood high in the community and might have been a rich man but for his kindness of heart. I expect if his old books could be found, they would tell a tale not pleasant for some of the early citizens' descendants to hear. He was prominent as a Mason and well beloved by everybody. His son Fred lives in Jefferson City now. He was a schoolmate of mine at the old Hereford school but was younger and the most I knew of him has been learned in later years. Until he became paralyzed, he was a useful citizen and if ever anyone thought ill of Fred, they kept it to themselves. The next house on that side of the street was B. H. McCarty's livery stable. It stood were the present United States court house know is.

I now come to one of the most noted characters that ever lived in Jefferson City, B. H. McCarty. Everybody, white and black, liked Burr McCarty. He was fond of horses and kept a livery stable as much

---

* Frazier

for the ability it gave him to keep fine horses as he did for the profit it brought. He was never known to keep for any length of time an inferior animal. He had a fine horse that he called Black Hawk that could make the best time of any race horse in the country. He was a little inclined to be superstitious and believed in ghosts as nearly everyone did who was raised in the days of slavery. On a certain day, there was to be a circus in town and Mr. McCarty found himself shorter in the hay line than he was willing to risk on show day. So he got up before day and mounted Black Hawk and rode to Miller's creek to where he knew there was hay for sale. He saw the man that owned the hay and made arrangements to have him bring it to town in time for the show.

BURR HARRISON MCCARTY

In this same valley, a short time before a man by the name of Burr had been hung for the murder of his wife. Mr. McCarty on his return home happened to think of the hanging and looking over that way, he thought he saw Burr hanging from the gallows. Thinking of ghosts, he became frightened and said he expected Burr to jump up behind him every minute. He put the whip to Black Hawk and he said no better time was ever made by him until he reached the stable and when he jumped off him, he confidently expected to see Burr's ghost sitting astride of Black Hawk behind the saddle. Once or twice on the way in, he thought he felt Burr's arms gripping him around the waist. After daylight, he concluded he would measure the length of Black Hawk's leaps and he declared they were over twenty feet in length.

Mr. McCarty had some very original expressions and they were very descriptive in their effect. One or two of them come to mind at this time. In Virginia, where he came from, there were a great many mullen stalks. They grew very tall and were of varied thickness. Some were stout and strong and others were thin and bent very easily. There was a small bird in that region named a killadover. These birds roosted in the mullen stalks. When Mr. McCarty wished to emphasize his appreciation of a friend, he would say: "He is a mullen stalk that will do to roost on." When he doubted the ability of his friends or neighbors to accomplish what they were undertaking or about to undertake, he would exclaim: "He can't shingle through to cover a goose."

He was a great friend and admirer of mine when I was a boy and often talked to me about how a boy might succeed in life and make a man of himself. Once when I met him after being to college, he said: "Bob, they tell me that you are writing poetry!" I replied that sometimes I indulged the Muse. He then told me that there were two kinds of men that rarely succeeded in life - one who tried to write poetry and the other who tried to sing and lead a choir. He then told me a story of a party who lived in Virginia. He said there was a young man there that persisted in going to see a widow's daughter when the mother had indicated many times that she did not want him to come to the house. He was addicted to writing what he believed was poetry. One cold, blustery day in winter he called on the object of his affections and took with him some of his manuscript and read with great gusto to the young lady. Cold as the weather was, he had on linen breeches. While he was in the height of his reading, the old lady came in. Her daughter exclaimed: "Mother, you ought to listen to some of the beautiful poetry George is reading to me and he composed it himself." The old lady said: "I can write poetry, too." He was surprised to hear that his prospective mother-in-law was a votary of the Muses and insisted that she give them a specimen of her production. The old lady glanced at his legs over the rims of her spectacles and said: "Linen breeches in winter!"

It was a long time after this story before I again mounted my *Pegasus* and the few times that I have found myself astride of him, I have called to mind the story of my early friend and have quickly dismounted.

Across the street from the McCarty livery stable was the house now occupied by Dr. J. L. Thorpe [111 E. High]. I do not remember who lived in it at the period of which I am writing but at one time it was kept by "Uncle" Hal Dixon. It was then called the City Hotel. My father put up at this hostelry when he first came to Jefferson City in 1837. In the fall of 1840, my father rented it and kept it until the spring of 1841 when he failed in the hotel business and was compelled to go back to building houses. The legislature in those years met in November and my father opened this hotel to receive them. He had to get his flour from [illegible] the nearest point at which it could be obtained. All the other supplies except meat had to be shipped from St. Louis and they had to be obtained before the river froze. My father had made great preparations expecting to fill his house with members of the legislature. For some reason that he could not just understand, he never more than half filled it. And spring found him ruined in fortune but not in spirit. He soon struggled again towards the front and ever afterwards kept well up with the procession.

In those days, as in these, all hotels kept a bar and to give some idea of how cheap liquors were in those days, my father used to fill a jug, in which "Uncle" Hal Dixon would send him buttermilk, with whiskey and return it and both thought it a fair exchange.

R. E. Young

A CHARIVARI
HOW GEN. BOLTON AND WIFE TRIED TO ESCAPE ONE

THE MISSOURI STATE TRIBUNE, SATURDAY EVENING APRIL 27, 1901
PAGE 1, COLUMNS 1-2

To the Editor of the State Tribune:

There was at the time of which I write a two-story stone house back of the Neef residence. It was occupied by the Lusk family consisting of a widow, two daughters, and two sons. The father of this family died before I was old enough to remember. He came from Virginia among the first settlers of the place and I think he was a printer.* When I first remember the family, James, the elder son, was editor and publisher of the *Jefferson City Inquirer* and William, the youngest, was connected with the paper in some capacity. After James' death, which occurred in the 50s, William took full charge of the paper and conducted it until the war began when he raised a battalion of cavalry on the Union side of the controversy and went away in the war.

The *Inquirer* was a staunch supporter of Col. Benton until the campaign of 1860 when it became a Republican paper and supported Abe Lincoln for the presidency. James Lusk was just the opposite of his brother William in their youthful days. James was very quiet and steady while William was inclined to be wild.

This brings me to the point where I can describe a coterie of people who were in the days of their glory, so to speak, years before. It consisted of Wm. Lusk, Thaddeus Boone, P. T. Miller, Ben and George B. Winston, Eph Ewing, Ben Gunn, Al Daber, Shelton, Burch, Eph Burr, Pope Dorris, and one or two others whose names I cannot just now call to mind. The youths of this day and generation are not "in it" with those of the early "forties." I was always fond of Mr. P. T. Miller as indeed was everybody else that knew him.

He told me of many of the wild pranks of the above named coterie, one of which I distinctly remember. I think it occurred during Christmas week as halloween was not considered in those days. They

---

* William Lusk, Sr. and his wife, Mary Fitzsimmons, were natives of Pennsylvania and had eight children

took a wagon from the shop of George Owens which was on the lot where D. C. Weatherby is now building a new store house and carried it to the locust grove back of where the Monroe House and other buildings on High street now stand and piece by piece carried it up to the top of two locust trees and put it together up there. Next day, it was the wonder of the town how that wagon got up in those trees. John Owens obligated himself not to prosecute the parties who put the wagon there if they would take it down again. On New Year's morning, at the close of the holidays, the wagon was in Owens' shop and it was a long time before it was known who were the guilty parties.

WILLIAM H. LUSK

These young gentlemen were in the habit of blackening any countryman who came to town and got drunk enough to fall by the wayside. There was in the county a man by the name of Hunter who was in the habit of "loading up" when he came to town but never got drunk enough to not be able to ride home. He was very indignant that a neighbor of his had been blackened and swore that there were not enough men in the town to black him. One day he came to town and got into a "meaning way" and on his rounds of the saloons, which were not so numerous as now, he ran across Thad. Boone, the dare-devil of the town. Thad. told him he would stand by him and the two could clean out the town if necessary. There were no street lamps in those days and when it did get dark, it was about equal to the Egyptian variety.

In the rounds, Thad. managed to have one of the boys slip into his left hand a batch of printers ink. After dark set and as they were passing the entrance of what is now known as Hog Alley from Madison street, Thad. slapped him in the face and eyes with his left hand and gave it such a swipe as to cover his whole face with printers' ink and quick as thought disappeared down the alley. When Hunter realized what had happened, he struck a bee line for his horse. It was a long time before Hunter was again seen in town and when he did come, Thad. hid out until he was gone.

Charivaris were common in those days and no widow nor widower escaped this coterie of youths if they had the temerity to get married in Jefferson City. There was a gentleman, Gen. Bolton by name, who married the Widow Chase of Callaway. Gen. Bolton lived on the Osage some ten or twelve miles from town and had been a widower for several years. He and the Widow Chase married in Callaway county and took a boat for St. Louis. They thought when they would return after their honeymoon some weeks later that they would escape the dreaded charivari but they were mistaken. The General had ordered his carriage to meet him at the wharf at the foot of Jefferson street. The "boys" were on the lookout and blockaded Madison and High streets at their junction with goods boxes. At that time there was no other way to reach Gen. Bolton's home from the steamboat landing. When the carriage reached the blockade, the "boys" seized the horses and quickly unhitched them from the carriage and hauled the carriage with the boys' pants up and down the streets in the worst din that was ever heard in Christendom. Gen. Bolton was furious at first and the widow was badly frightened but he soon saw the only way there was out of the trouble and called to the boys to stop at the first saloon and drink it dry if they wanted to and he would foot the bill. It was said that the next night the boys hired a band and went out and serenaded the couple and partook of a hearty supper which the bride had provided for them.

Besides the two Lusk boys, there were two girls, Misses Martha and Mary Ann. Miss Martha died of cholera in the epidemic of 1850 or 1851. From what I heard my mother say of her, she was a most estimable lady. She was a fast friend of my aunt, Miss Ellen Dillinger* and frequently visited at our house. Miss Mary Ann was a long resident of this city and known to a large circle of friends still living in Jefferson City.

Nearly opposite the Lusk residence was the Virginia Hotel now the Central Hotel. When I first remember it, there was nothing of it except the walls and the roof. The floors were not laid and we boys played over the joists at the risk of breaking our necks. The hotel was built and owned by Gen. Thomas L. Price and the first man that kept hotel there was Wm. D. Kerr. He was a prince among Benefices and very popular as an innkeeper and citizen. He had married the Widow Callahan who was a daughter of Michael Newman, the keeper of the City Hotel formerly the Paulsel House. She made a splendid landlady, having been brought up to the business as it were. When she and Mr. Kerr were married, they each possessed a child by their former marriage, Miss Mollie Callahan afterwards Mrs. Wm. E. Miller and Lucius Kerr. Miss Mollie was a very pretty girl and Lucius was a fine-looking young man. He was a steamboat pilot, a very fascinating profession in those days. It was said of him and Bill Miller, another Jefferson City boy, that they could pilot a boat from St. Louis to Fort Leavenworth without touching a sandbar or striking a snag. Lucius Kerr was the author of the saying that "water was only fit for two things, cattle to drink and steamboats to float in." Lucius Kerr was a very wild youth but one of the wittiest men Jefferson City ever produced. He was tall and slender in build with black hair and black eyes and although petted by all, especially the girls, he never became spoiled but was always the same congenial, good-natured fellow. I do not know what became of him. His father, after quitting the hotel business, was for many years the city clerk and died in the city loved and respected by everybody.   ***R. E. Young***

---

* Dellinger

FOOLED HIS WIFE
HOW DR. POPE DORRIS ATTENDED A BALL

THE MISSOURI STATE TRIBUNE, SATURDAY EVENING MAY 4, 1901
PAGE 1, COLUMNS 1-2

To the Editor of the State Tribune:

In the house now occupied by Charles Maus' store on the [northeast] corner of High and Jefferson streets lived Levi Gunsaullis.* He was sheriff and collector of Cole county at the time of which I write and had been elected by the anti-Benton Democracy. After his term of office expired, he moved to St. Louis and I lost sight of him.

Opposite this house on High street and a little east of it stood the Jefferson House. It was kept by John D. Curry and in its day and generation was counted a first-class hostelry. Their family, as well as I can remember, consisted of two sons, Dr. William Curry, John Curry and a niece, Miss Bettie Bohanan. Dr. Curry practiced his profession in Jefferson City for several years, perhaps until 1856 or '57 when he went into a land speculation with Col. [James B.] Gardenhire and others and bought or got options on all the land between the water tower and Gray's creek. This body of land was called Upper Jefferson. A large business house or two were erected at Gray's creek and immediately went into "innocuous desuetude." The land eventually went into the hands of its original owners and the Jefferson City Land Company went broke. The Doctor was as far as I know a successful practitioner of medicine but visionary in business matters.

John Curry helped about the hotel but was as I remember, inclined to be wild and "ne'er do well." Miss Bettie Bohanan was a beautiful girl as I remember and married a lawyer of St. Louis of considerable distinction whose name does not now occur to me. Mrs. Curry was a splendid landlady and was one of the characters of Jefferson City. She came from Culpepper county, Virginia which fact you would learn in a two minutes' conversation with her. There was nothing that could be made nor anything that could grow equal to the products of Culpepper county, Virginia. She told my mother who was a Washington county Marylander that if she wanted to make the nicest

---

* Gunsallus

preserves that she could imagine, that she would loan her a brass kettle that she brought from Culpepper county, Virginia. Mother declined the generous offer and denied herself the luxury of eating such delicious preserves for fear the famous kettle might get damaged in her hands and the art forever lost. I don't think that she and mother ever came to any agreement when the advantages of Washington county, Maryland and Culpepper county, Virginia were up for discussion although at other times they were good friends and companionable.

Her most known accomplishment was her fondness for and ability to talk. She could beat anybody talking in Jefferson City in her day and generation and although we have some fine talkers now whose reputation will go down to posterity in poetry and prose, still I know of no one that can equal Mrs. Curry. Dr. Lynn, who boarded with her, used to tell a story which he declared was true as Holy Writ and which I never heard her deny. [He said] there was a lady stopping at the hotel from Culpepper county, Virginia and that she and Mrs. Curry got into a quiet discussion in the parlor when he left in the morning and kept it up until he returned in the night. Next morning after breakfast, he looked in the parlor before going to his office and saw this lady guest on the floor and Mrs. Curry whispering in her ear. Mrs. Curry was a most estimable lady and a good neighbor. As Col. Levi Gunsaullis[*] used to say in speaking of the Curry family: "The gray mare was the best horse in that team.

Across the street next to the Gunsaullis'[*] house lived a Mrs. Sharp. Her residence was about where Gus Fischer's drug store now is [105 E. High]. She was in a lawsuit of some destitution in which Capt. M. M. Parsons was counsel on the other side. She was a witness in the case and Capt. Parsons was noted for his severity with a witness that was testifying against him. He removed her gloves, so to speak, when she was on the stand and in passing her house the next day, she waylaid him and took occasion to slap his face. He went away from her as quickly as he could exclaiming: "I cannot defend myself against a woman."

In those days, there was a drug store in this neighborhood kept by Dr. [Alexander] Pope Dorris and I think Gen. Jackson L. Smith was the drug clerk, then a youth of 15 or 16 summers. It was the common resort for nearly all the men in town for Dr. Dorris, besides

[*] Gunsallus

being a good physician, was a most companionable gentleman. I know many good stories in which Dr. Dorris figured as the chief character. His wife was a daughter of Squire Carr, the tinner of the town. She was a good, consistent Methodist and the Doctor leaned toward that persuasion himself but he was so full of frolic and such a genial fellow that it was a hard matter to keep him up to the "scratch." He was a fine singer and when he attended church, always led the singing. His wife could manage him as long as she had him within the sphere of her influence but when the Doctor got away from her, he was about as wild as a colt that had never been bridled. He was fond of going to dances, picnics, and other places where there was merry-making.

Once upon a time, there was a ball at Cedar City in the times when the Chappells, Smiths, and Tarltons held the sway in that region. The Doctor wanted to go and at the same time he knew his good wife would strenuously oppose his going. The Marshal of the town was a boon companion and fast friend of the Doctor's. So in the afternoon of the day the ball was to come off, he asked Bill Rhodes, the Marshal, if he would do him a favor. Bill replied that he would do anything within his power. "Well," said the Doctor, "I want to go to that ball at Cedar City tonight and if Jane, my wife, suspicions that I want to go, she will just raise Cain. Now, Bill, what I want you to do is to come to my house about 9 o'clock and call me up. I'll go to bed early and complain that I am awfully tired and sleepy. I want you to tell my wife when she comes to the door that there has been a terrible fight at the ball over at Cedar and that a man has been cut and is bleeding terribly and they want me to come as soon as possible and that Phil. Chappell is waiting with a skiff at Rogers' landing." Rhodes promised and at the appointed time he knocked at the Doctor's door. Mrs. Dorris went to the door (the Doctor had already retired and appeared to be sound asleep). When the good wife heard Rhodes story, she called the Doctor but he appeared so sound asleep that she went to the bed and shook him. He seemed to be about half awake when he demanded to know what was the matter. Mrs. Dorris hurriedly told him and insisted that he get up at once as the man might bleed to death. "Let the trifling dog bleed to death," growled the Doctor. "You don't care a cent how tired I am just so I am going all the time and making money for you and Thom to spend." However, she prevailed and he got up to dress when she admonished him about wearing his everyday clothes to a ball where he would meet the

Chappells and Tarltons in their best attire and got out his Sunday suit for him and insisted that he wear it. He obeyed her as he always did, grumbling all the while. At last he was off with Rhodes following close at his heels. When they turned the first corner on the journey, the Doctor jumped up and cracked his heels together exclaiming: "Whoop'e! Out till day!" Mrs. Dorris never could find out who the man was that was so dangerously wounded.

When the War Between the States was on, Doctor Dorris, true to his southern ancestry and to his training, went with the south. He was surgeon of Parsons' Brigade and did splendid service at Carthage, Wilson's Creek, Lexington, and Pea Ridge. After the battle of Pea Ridge, he saved my life by his skillful treatment and patient care. On the retreat from that battle, from exposure and a previous attack of pneumonia, I had a violent hemorrhage of the lungs and all my friends despaired of my recovery. But the Doctor stuck to me closer than a mother and here I am today while my faithful and skillful friend is gathered with his fathers. The Doctor had a son, Thomas, who was with us in the war and a faithful and gallant soldier. He returned after the war but died somewhere in the south when he went to retrieve the fortunes of his family. The Doctor practiced several years after the war in Callaway county. He was always a successful practitioner but never knew the value of money so between his generosity and poor collections he died comparatively poor.

R. E. Young

OLDEN TIMES
A STORY TOLD ON DR. TENNESSEE MATHEWS

THE MISSOURI STATE TRIBUNE, SATURDAY EVENING MAY 11, 1901
PAGE 1 , COLUMNS 1-2

To the Editor of the State Tribune:

Next door east of Dr. Dorris' drug store lived Mr. Peter
Miller. I think he was a cooper by trade but when I first remember
him, he had a small grocery store and huckster stand at the place above
named. He had three sons and two daughters as I remember the
family. Two of the sons, John and Jacob, are yet living in Jefferson
City. Fred was the oldest and occupied the position now held by Col.
Buehrle. He fired all the salutes on the Fourth of July and
Washington's Birthday, which, with the celebration of the victory at
New Orleans, were the only occasions when salutes were fired.
During one of these celebrations, Fred was powder-burned so that he
lost one of his eyes and I think one of his hands was badly crippled.
During the war of the rebellion, this family was very loyal and in their
zeal for the cause, they became estranged from many of their former
friends.

Mr. Peter Miller was a very earnest Baptist and worshipped in
the old Baptist Church on Miller and Monroe streets now occupied by
the colored people. There was a good story told of him and Dr.
Mathews who was also a Baptist. It seems they sat together on the
front seat and raised the tune as was common in all the churches of
those days when there was no regular choir nor organ. Dr. Mathews
had a [illegible] which he used for pitching the tune, as it was called.
On one occasion the Doctor pitched the tune and Brother Miller, who
spoke broken English, said: "Doctor you got dot tune just a little too
high." The Doctor then pitch a tune lower **and Miller again
interrupted: "a little to low, doctor." Dr. Mathews turned fiercely
on Miller and shouted: "Sing it yourself, damn you!"**[*]

[This portion of the paper has been damaged and is illegible - ed.]

---

[*] Boldface words adapted from similar story of Julius H. Conrath in James E. Ford's *A
History of Jefferson City* published by The New Day Press of Jefferson City in 1938.

...it was a new experience to me and I was at a loss how to wash clothes as any other boy who had been raised in a southern home.

We were camped on the Osage river in St. Clair county and I took my dirty clothes down to the river [illegible]. "Uncle Jake" came and asked me what I was trying to do. When he found out that [illegible] in the future, as long as he was in reach of us, he would wash his clothes and mine if I would get the wood and water and hang up the clothes. It was a bargain and we both lived up to it when we were together. Sometimes I had the best of the trade and sometimes he had; owing to the proximity of the wood and water to camp.

Once when we were in camp at Arkadelphia, Ark., he bought all the flour at a certain mill for the use of headquarters and put a guard over it. Our battery of artillery was camped near the place with two brigades of infantry. One night while the guards slept, the flour was stolen. The next day an official search was ordered and Major [John B.] Ruthven, the Commissary, with other officers made a close search of our battery quarters. None of the flour was found. After the search was over, "Uncle Jake" came to our camp and said: "Boys, I know you stole that flour because no other company would have dared to steal it." He was right. We had gone there at night and found the guard asleep and sack by sack carried it out. When we got to camp, we dug a hole in the ground under each camp fire and buried it. When all the excitement was over and Major Ruthven reported that the flour could not be found, we brought it forth and sent "Uncle Jake" a large mess of it. He said he was proud of his "boys;" that if they did steal the flour, they had sense enough not to be caught.

At one time when I was greatly in need of a pair of pantaloons, I asked "Uncle Jake" if he could not find me a pair somewhere. A few days after, he brought me a pair of gray jeans-breeches. He said that a lady had made them for her son who was in the 19th Louisiana and before she could send them, her son was killed in battle. She told him she wanted to give them to a needy soldier who was worthy and "Uncle Jake," in presenting them to me, said: "I know you will never disgrace them." "Uncle Jake" lived to return home and some years ago died in Vernon county, Mo., well-to-do, honored, and loved by all who knew him.

Somewhere close to the Peter Miller residence, there was a saddler shop owned and operated by a Mr. Magerley. He lived in the little frame house now standing on the alley north of the courthouse.

My memory of him is kept green by the fact that he made me the first saddle I ever owned. After my father ordered it, I was in his shop two or three times daily until it was completed. My friend Jacob Straus, now of St. Louis, learned the trade with him. I do not know what became of Mr. Magerley or just when he left Jefferson City.

My friend Jacob Straus was in the army of the Confederate States with me and is now the principal owner of the Straus Saddle and Harness Company of St. Louis. I remember a good story on Jake when we were boys. We were both going to school to Hazel Burlingame and at what is now known as "Hobo Hill"...

[Rest of letter is illegible - ed.]

The following is credited to Dr. Young's series of letters by James E. Ford in *A History of Jefferson City* published by the New Day Press of Jefferson City 1938. The date of this letter's publication is unknown as Ford did not directly cite his sources. It is likely that Ford paraphrased Dr. Young as have other authors.

Citizens would congregate at the post office about four o'clock in the afternoon for the mail from St. Louis. My impression is that it was a daily mail, not oftener than that. The mail came in a stage coach drawn by four horses. Behind the driver's seat was a leather contrivance called the boot. In this was transported the mail and baggage if any while the body of the vehicle was reserved for passengers. Six people could ride inside. If there were any more they were either seated with the driver outside or on top with the extra baggage. The driver carried slung over his shoulder a long tin winding horn or bugle. As the people congregated at the post office, they listened for the bugle note of the driver as he reached Boggs' Hill about a mile and a half east of town.

Business men left their stores or counting rooms, maidens with their beaux stood at a respectful distance from the crowd while everybody peered into the coach to see if they might know the travelers or if any friend for whom they were looking had come. Presently the four or six horses would sweep by in a trot, the coach would come to a stop while the tired travelers would tumble out and the mail was dragged into the hotel office or post office. As the mail was opened, the mail clerk would call out who the letters were for. Some of the more pretentious people had boxes but the great majority got their mail through public delivery.

AN XMAS SCRAP
THAT OCCURRED MORE THAN FIFTY YEARS AGO

THE MISSOURI STATE TRIBUNE, SATURDAY EVENING JUNE 8, 1901
PAGE 1, COLUMNS 1-2

To the Editor of the State Tribune:

In the house now occupied by H. B. Church, Sr. [304 Madison], there was a saloon in the years about which I am writing. I do not know who kept it but it was here where the celebrated McDaniel Dorris whiskey was kept. It was as clear as spring water and was made by McDaniel Dorris of Jefferson City. McD. Dorris also made peach brandy and apple-jack. Someone not drunk, and I think it was Judge Clay Ewing who twitted Dorris for making such liquors, said that if a man got drunk on it, it took a week to get sober again. Dorris said he must have drank a large portion, for his whisky was as innocent as the same quantity of buttermilk. In these days, Mr. Dorris could make and sell any amount of his liquors for, as he said, there was no "infernal revenue tax to bother a man."

At this saloon one Christmas Eve night, I saw the worst personal experience that I remember to have ever seen. As was customary in those days, we had a bonfire made of logs of wood and fed by dried leaves in the place occupied by the intersection of High and Madison streets. Here all the boys of the town, white and black, assemble to shoot guns, pistols, and explode fire crackers.

The men were going and coming out of the above referred to saloon when someone yelled "fight." Of course we boys ran there to see it. If there is anything that occurs on the earth which will attract boys, or men for that matter, as is a fight, I do not know of it. When we got there, we found the fight was between Jim Sone, father of our present collector, and Floyd Crandell,* a farmer living a few miles west of the town. Neither man had ever been whipped and both had a fine reputation as fighters. I don't think anyone ever knew what they fought about, though it was probably McDaniel Dorris' whiskey. Crandell* began the fight by hitting Sone in the forehead with the butt end of a pistol. I remember when they were parted by mutual friends,

---

* Crandall

that both looked like they had been drunk and hog killing. Both claimed that if the friends had not interfered, the other would have gotten the soundest thrashing ever heard of.

On the corner where Abe Heim's store is [site of Exchange National Bank], a man by the name of Thalheimer kept a general merchandise establishment. He was a pretty fair dealer; so I heard mother say but was inclined to talk cross, especially if one did not buy of him after having him show his goods. Ladies in these days were not entirely different from what they are today in shopping. They often looked at about everything there is in the store before they purchased and would be exasperating to the salesman by buying a yard of ribbon or going out without buying anything. Now I know, every lady who reads this will say: "That is so with nearly all the women but I never do that-a-way."

It was on such occasions that our friend Thalheimer would get out of humor and "sass back" at the ladies. One day when he was especially in a bad humor, Mrs. Dr. William Davison came in and whether nor not she bought anything, I do not know. But Thalheimer said something that wounded her feelings and she went out and told her husband. Dr. William Davison was ordinarily a quiet and mild mannered man, almost the counterpart of his brother "Sandy," as Dr. Alex. M. Davison was familiarly called. On this occasion, he lost his temper and rushing into Thalheimer's store, he picked up an ax or hatchet and proceeded to clear the establishment. It was said that Thalheimer hid under the counter behind a sugar barrel. When the belligerent doctor found he had no foe worthy of his steel, he began to laugh and left the house.

To give you some idea of the difference in manner between these Drs. Davison, although brothers, I will relate an incident of their lives told me by my mother. It seems Dr. William had wounded his hand with a file and it became very much inflamed, so much so that at one time it looked like he would lose his arm if not his life. Every boy friend of his in town called to see him and he was very popular with the women and children on account of his mildness in manner. Every lady had some remedy to offer that had proved successful in her experience.

[This portion of the paper is illegible]

Dr. William [Davison] owned a farm about two miles west of town and the latter part of his life was spent there. He had a mania for attending sales and buying many things for which apparently he had no use. Once, after the war, I stayed all night at his house and in the morning, he took me about the farm showing me his stock and growing crops. As we passed through the barnyard, I saw parts of several old machines lying around. I asked him where he got them. He said he had bought them at different sales. I wanted to know what he intended to do with them. He laughed and said: "There are many bolts and pieces of iron that come in handy on a farm like this. I can find something in these old scraps to mend a broken tool which if I did not have, I would have to make a trip to town to get." I said no more but wondered if he could not keep an assortment of bolts to be obtained at the hardware store that would cost less.

He was in his day and time a surgeon and physician, wealthy, and I never heard anyone speak ill of Dr. Wm. Davison. He was gentle and tender. Although not our family doctor, he was a bosom friend of my father and gave me many words of advice and encouragement.

[The rest of this issue is damaged and is illegible, see page 161 - ed.]

NEWMAN'S
CITY HOTEL

HENRY PAULSEL
A HIGHLY POLISHED GENTLEMAN STOOD BY A FRIEND

THE MISSOURI STATE TRIBUNE, SATURDAY EVENING JUNE 15, 1901
PAGE 1, COLUMNS 1-2

To the Editor of the State Tribune:

The Paulsel house mentioned in my last letter is represented by the present City Hotel [site of Central Trust Bank]. The office of the Paulsel house was where Straub's cigar store is now. The landlord of the hotel was Henry Paulsel. He was very popular and a man of polished manners but high-tempered and prided himself in determination to stand by his friends. Once when two prominent citizens were quarreling in the post office and about to come to blows, he stepped up behind his friend and dropped a Derringer pistol in his friend's pocket. The gentleman facing him seeing the procedure cried out: "I am unarmed." Paulsel then got between them and asked his friend to desist. When the Paulsel house passed into the possessions of the Newmans, it changed to City Hotel and has since been known by that name. This family, as I remember it, consisted of the father Michael, the brother Harding, and two or three sisters - Mrs. Callahan afterwards Mrs. Kerr, Miss Maggie, and Mrs. Kingsberry. They kept a good hotel and were still in charge of the house when the war began. Mr. Kingsberry was a very mild tempered man. He died before I could remember but I heard my father recite incidents connected with his life that led me to believe that he almost had the patience of Job.

In this building where Miller's saloon now is, Charly Stewart and George W. Hough kept a general store and Fount[ain] McKenzie was the clerk. I have spoken of Mr. Hough before in these letters. If I remember correctly, Mr. Hough was one of the first members of the board of public works. The board is not now in existence and was abolished before the war.

Mr. Stewart was at one time factor of the penitentiary, an office now merged into that of warden. In those days the warden only had charge of the police regulations of the institution. The factor fed and clothed the prisoners and bought and sold everything brought into or taken out of the prison. The principal articles then manufactured in the penitentiary in its early days were barrels, wagons, and ropes. There was a great deal of hemp raised in the county and State in the early days of the penitentiary but after the war, hemp raising ceased and the manufacture of rope ceased also. During the move and freighting to California, the manufacture of wagons in the prison was quite a business. The making of barrels created quite a trade in stables and [illegible] in Cole, Osage, and Miller counties. Mr. Stewart was factor in [Austin A.] King's and [Sterling] Price's administrations and conducted the prison in economical matters.

Fount McKenzie had been orderly sergeant to Capt. Parson's company, Doniphan's regiment, in the war with Mexico. He made quite a record for gallantry in that war and was very popular while employed in Hough & Stewart's store. I think he went to California when the fever was on but returned and raised a company for Bob McCulloch's regiment of Confederates. I was a member of his company but was detailed as Gen. Parsons' orderly. I never knew much of Capt. McKenzie as a soldier although a member of his company. He fell in the battle of Carthage [on] July 5, 1861 leading his company into that town. Gen. Parsons revered his memory and after the battle buried him with the honors due his rank.

Back of the Hough & Stewart store was a little room now a part of the City Hotel office. In this room, Morris and Joe Obermayer made caps and I used to think they were the prettiest ones I ever saw. Their brother Simon and another brother whose name I cannot call to memory kept the store founded by them in 1844 on the corner now occupied by Weiser & Artz. In this store, Morris and Joe sold their caps. They afterwards bought Simon out - the other brother having died of cholera. Morris and Joe continued in this store until Morris died. Then Joe went to Kansas City and died there.

South of Thalheimer's store on Madison street was Dr. A. M. Davison's office. In those days, the drug store as a separate establishment was unknown. Every Dr. either compounded his own prescriptions or had a drug store in connection with his office. In this office of Dr. A. M. Davison, many young men of that day studied medicine. Among the number I remember was Sherwood Owens, William Curry, and Richard Wells. Sherwood Owens went to California with the gold fever but returned and is now living in Texas where he enjoyed a successful and reputable practice. Dr. Curry practiced here for several years and left the practice to enter business and was a public printer, banker, and land speculator. I think he now lives with his son in Kansas City.

Dr. Richard Wells went to the Mexican War in Capt. Parson's company. He was wounded in a personal encounter in the City of Mexico having a dirk driven through his neck. After he recovered, which was considered phenomenal [as] you could plainly see by the scars where the knife entered and then came out on the opposite side. It was often said that a skillful surgeon could hardly pass a knife through in the same manner without causing death.

After his return from Mexico, he practiced his profession in Jefferson City and was for some time a partner of Dr. G[eorge] B[ickerton] Winston. Dr. Wells was a very polished gentleman in his manners, always dressed well, and was fairly successful in his practice but for some inexplicable reason was not popular. He was said to be one of the best read persons in the town in his day. He was very fond of fishing and in the fishing season it was hard to find him at home. He was kind to children and most all of us boys in town loved him. I remember that once when the circus was in town, I had loaned one of the men a shovel to let me in the circus and afterwards could not find the shovel nor man. I met Dr. Wells and told him my troubles. He sympathized with me and said: "Boy, your shovel is perhaps lost but come with me. You shall see the circus." After the show was over, I went on a careful tour of inspection and succeeded in getting the shovel but I never did find the man that borrowed it.

Dr. Wells remained in Jefferson City during the war and was connected with one of the hospitals here. After the war, he found it impossible to make a living here in the practice of his profession and moved away to some of the Western States. He was a strong Union man but I never heard of his persecuting anyone. There was something strange about the sentiment that prevailed among southern people after the close of the war. They could fraternize with people who came among them from the North or who were citizens of the South before the war but nothing could make them chummy with those who were born and raised in the South and went against them in war.

A few doors south of Dr. Davison's office on Madison street was the residence and tin shop of Squire Clark of whom I will speak in my next.

R. E. Young

THE BATTLE OF HELENA

THE MISSOURI STATE TRIBUNE, SATURDAY EVENING JULY 6, 1901
PAGE 3 , COLUMNS 3-5

To the Editor of the State Tribune:

Instead of writing you my usual communication about Jefferson City in its earlier days, I thought it might interest your readers more in giving you a brief history of the battle of Helena, Arkansas as I saw it.

Our command had been all winter and spring in Little Rock recruiting, drilling, and organizing. Gen. [Sterling] Price had succeeded Gen. [Thomas C.] Hindman in command of our division which consisted of [Mosby Monroe] Parsons' brigade of Missouri and [Dandridge] McRae's brigade of Arkansas. We had marched northward to Jacksonport on White River believing we were on our way back to our beloved Missouri. Every morning our brigade started on the march to the tune of *"The Girl I Left Behind Me."* When we arrived at Jacksonport, we went into temporary camp calling it "Camp Stonewall Jackson" in honor of him who had recently fallen in defense of our cause.

After we had spent some days in drilling, organizing, and equipping our forces, we started for Helena on the Mississippi River. Gen. [Theophilus] Holmes was commander of the corps which was composed of Price's, [James S.] Fagan's, and Marmaduke's divisions of the Trans-Mississippi Department, C.S.A. In order to reach Helena, we had to cross Cash River* which at this season of the year was out of its banks. The land lying between Jackson[port] and Helena was low and flat and at that time was nearly covered with water from Cash* and White rivers which were both overflowed. We had a terrible time in crossing this flat overflowed country. We were without pontoons and had to improvise them in many places by rafts. Fortunately for us, the streams we had to cross are practically without current - the water moving so sluggishly that it was difficult to determine whether it moved at all or not. After many days of tedious marching through mud and water, we reached a point 14 miles south of Helena on the afternoon of the 3rd of July, 1863. Here we were ordered to go into camp and prepare three days rations for our haversacks. It was ascertained that on account of the roughness of the ground over which we would be compelled to march and owing to the fact that the Federals had cut the timber and thrown it across every avenue of approach, we would be unable to take any field artillery into the fight. A short time after our battery went into park, we received orders from headquarters to equip thirty-five men as sharpshooters with one lieutenant and to report them to Major [Lebbeus] Pindall who was in command of a battalion of sharpshooters. Capt. [Charles B.] Tilden who was at that time in command of our battery called for volunteers to make this detail. The whole company volunteered. The captain then detailed 35 men and one lieutenant to lot. The command of the detail fell upon Lieutenant A. A. Lesueur. We were then armed and reported to Major Pindall. Our guns were left in charge of Capt. Tilden and the remainder of the men and were not used in the battle at all the next day for the reasons above given.

An incident occurred at this juncture of our affairs which made a lasting impression upon my mind. One of our detail named [S.] Hagan had a presentiment that he would be killed in the coming battle. He had a cousin in the company named [Calom E.] Dawson who had escaped the detail.   He went to Dawson and told him of the

---

* Cache River

presentiment and asked him to take his place. Dawson was as brave a man as there was in the army but as he was not detailed, he did not care to hazard his life. He explained to Hagan that he would have to take his place in the line and the bullet that was to kill him (Hagan) would not spare him (Dawson) because of the change. Hagan said no more but went bravely into the battle and fell to rise no more in the first charge of the company. I never believed in presentiments but this was the best authenticated one that ever came to my knowledge.

We began our march with the sharpshooters at 12 o'clock of the night of the third of July in the following order: Pindall's sharpshooters in front followed by the 10th, 11th, and 16th Missouri regiments of infantry; the whole comprising Parsons' brigade of Price's division. Immediately in our front was McRae's brigade of Arkansas. They completed Price's division. On the march, Gen. Holmes and his staff passed us to an eminence from which as commander of the corps, he would be able to direct the battle. There were three forts with rifle pits protecting Helena in our front with a large bastion fort in the edge of Helena so placed as to protect the three outlying fortifications. The enemy's line might be very well described by a horse shoe or perhaps better by a crescent. The right prong of the crescent facing us had a strong fortification against which Gen. Marmaduke with his division was to be hurled. Price's division was to attack the center of the crescent which was protected by a sand-bag fort with rifle pits in front and located in a graveyard and called "graveyard fort." The enemy's left or the other prong of the crescent was armed with a sand-bag fort with rifle pits in front. Gen. Fagan with his division was ordered against this position. At daybreak, we were ordered to halt and load. The ground over which we were expected to fight was composed of high hills with deep ravines between them. The ground at one time had been heavily timbered. This timber the enemy had cut down and left lying on the ground. Over this uneven surface we were expected to charge and dislodge the enemy from his strong position. I shall not attempt to describe the part of any command in this memorable battle save that of Gen. Price. The "graveyard fort" was considered the key to the situation and against this our gallant Missourians and Arkansans were hurled. It must be remembered that immediately in rear of "graveyard fort" was Fort Curtis, a bastion fort in the edge of Helena. In addition to this fort, there was a gunboat in the river commanding the entire field.

About sunrise, we had reached a ridge about a quarter of a mile in front of "graveyard fort." On this ridge, we were ordered to lie down. Between us and the fort was a deep ravine filled with large trees thrown in almost every conceivable manner that would retard the advance of an enemy. While I was lying there on my breast, I had a good survey of what was before me. It was the Fourth of July. That glorious Fourth which I had so often celebrated in my Missouri home with firecrackers in my childhood and cannon in more mature years. There floated the stars and stripes which I had been taught was the emblem of freedom but upon which I now looked as the ensign of oppression. I wondered what would be the issue of this battle to me and my country. I never doubted for one moment that we would take that fort before us bristling with cannon and filled with exultant Yankees.

Our formation was what at that time [was] known as columns of divisions. That is, each company was divided into two equal parts and one placed directly in front of the other. The command was divided into several of these columns, one or two regiments in each. Our column was composed of Pindall's battalion of which our detail was a part and the 10th and 16th Missouri infantry. Capt. [Amos F.] Cake's company of Pindall's battalion in two divisions was in front of Lesueur's detachment which composed the third division in the column.

After we had lain there on our faces long enough to get somewhat rested, the command came: "Forward, double quick - charge." And at them we went with our "rebel yell." Down the declivity in front of us, across the ravine, and up the slope to the "graveyard fort" was the act of but a few minutes. Many a gallant Missourian went down to rise no more. As we were ascending the slope in front, my left hand file, Smith Thomas of Callaway, fell shot in the shoulder and my right hand file, Bill Boldridge from somewhere in North Missouri, fell wounded in the arm. On we went until we reached the rifle pits in front of the fort when the enemy, afraid of our glittering bayonets, fled pell-mell. So great was their rout that as they passed through the fort, they threw their entire force into a panic. We followed them shooting and keeping up our demoniac yelling until they found refuge under the banks of the Mississippi River. Then it was that the entire force of the other three federal forts was turned against our gallant band. Both Marmaduke and Fagan had failed in their attempt to take the positions assigned them. With these odds against us, we were forced back into the fort we had just taken. We held this position for six mortal hours against a force far superior to our own and would have been surrounded and captured only for a gallant act of Capt. Celsus Price. The enemy had left one road open which passed through "graveyard fort." This road was exposed to every gun in the three remaining forts. Gen. Price saw our situation and knew we would never retreat until ordered to do so and so he sent his son Capt. Price with orders to us to fall back. Along this road more than a quarter of a mile, he rode like the wind and when the order was delivered, he returned along the same road exposed to the entire fire of the enemy. How he escaped God only knows.

Many instances of heroism fell under my observation and some ridiculous incidents. After we had driven the enemy behind the banks of the river and were forced to fall back to the protection of the sand-bags which we had previously captured, Lieut. Lesueur ordered us to use a gun abandoned by the enemy. Enough of us to properly man the gun immediately laid hold of it. We found it shotted, that is the enemy had forced a ball home without any powder behind it. While we were trying to extricate the ball, the enemy's gunboat,[*] which by this time had moved to the opposite side of the river in full view of our position, opened fire on us. And it was not long until she got our range and threw a sixty-pound shell under the gun we were trying to use. There were nine of us at the gun when the shell exploded including Lieut. Lesueur. When the dust and smoke had cleared away, there was only John Waller of St. Charles and myself on our feet and we were covered with dirt and burnt powder. Waller had a quarter section of his pants torn away but was not otherwise damaged. I alone remained without damage to skin or clothing. Lieut. Lesueur was wounded in the leg below the knee but not seriously. Two of the number were killed and five wounded. At another time, my left hand file was wounded in the breast and died in the hospital. At another time, while two of us were protecting ourselves behind a stump down near the river, it was suddenly discovered that our position was untenable for the enemy was out flanking us on both flanks. We both retired. My comrade fell with a broken thigh while the God of battles again preserved me.

---

[*] The *U. S. S. Tyler*; The commander James M. Pritchett reported firing 413 rounds.

One of the ridiculous incidents I remember was a lieutenant with drawn sword standing behind a pile of sand-bags urging his men to sally forth and drive back the advancing foe. One of his men cried out to him: "Get from behind that sand-bag you d___ coward and we will follow you!"

Our retreat was almost as hazardous as our advance for the enemy with victory in view were crowding us on every side. Yet we sullenly retired disputing every inch of ground with them until we reached the protection of timber. It was a well-known fact, throughout our portion of the army at least, that the "Yanks" were loath to follow the "Johnnies" into the brush. Once in the brush, we scattered in squads and thus reached camp some two or three miles from Helena. Several of us found a spring and after quenching our thirst, formed a squad with Jim Woods as leader. This quasi organization proceeded to find our camp.

Why Gen. Holmes fought this battle I never was able to discover. It was said it was to relieve Vicksburg. Perhaps it was but Vicksburg fell the same day and Gettysburg was lost to us the day before.

We called this a bloody battle. Our brigade took 2,200 fighting men and officers into action; 250 of this number was captured; of the remainder, 650 were killed or left wounded on the field leaving 1300 to answer roll call [the] next day.

In reading of the late war in Cuba including Fort El-Canay, our veterans of the Civil War smile at the thought of there being any battles in Cuba. In our minds there was nothing occurred in the Spanish-American War that rose above a skirmish when compared with the fighting in the Civil War.

R. E. Young

OLD-TIMERS
PERPETUAL MOTION MADE A POOR MAN OF JNO. BAUER

THE MISSOURI STATE TRIBUNE, SATURDAY EVENING JULY 13, 1901
PAGE 1, COLUMNS 1-2

To the Editor of the State Tribune:

In my last communication on the early citizens of Jefferson City, I spoke of a gentleman who was well-known to many who are yet left from those early days but from a misspelling of his name I don't think many recognized the man. I hope we will get it correctly in this letter. The name of the man was Barcroft and not Bancroft as it read in my letter. He was a surveyor and helped to survey the state as its section and township lines now exist. A large part of the state had been surveyed by the French and they used "Arpent" which is about five-sevenths less in size than the English acre in measuring the land.

After leaving the corner now occupied by the Young Grocery company and continuing on the same side of the street, the first house you would come to in the days of which I write would be on the spot now occupied by Grimshaw Bros. In this frame building was a jeweler and watchmaker by the name of John Bauer. He was a man of more than average intelligence and a Mason in high standing. I have often stood at his window and wondered how he could take all those little wheels and things out of a watch and find enough places to put them in. He lived for many years in Jefferson City and would have been a wealthy man but in the latter part of his life, he conceived the idea that he could make perpetual motion which ruined him mentally and financially.

Across the street from Bauer's establishment was a log house weather-boarded that stood a little back from the street. Here that good man and lawyer Geo. T. White lived or rather had his office. His sign was on a board cut to represent an open book and across its pages was written *George T. White, attorney at law.* Geo. White grew up in Jefferson City. He was the nephew of Judge Thompkins of the Supreme Court who lived opposite Binder's park on the California road. I do not remember Judge Thompkins but often heard my father speak of him. George White was a promising young lawyer when he started out in life and for many years held a prominent position here at the bar. I have often heard my old friend Judge E. L. Edwards say that White was an excellent associate in a case for hunting up law points. Mr. White had some eccentric characteristics which made him a noted man about Jefferson. He told a good story and when he reached the laughing point, he would cut up some antics that were quite as laughable as the story he told.

He was also noted for his chirography. It was told of him that once he was away from home and wrote his wife to sell some stock he had on his farm. The story goes that when he returned, she showed him the letter and that he remarked people ought to write so other people could read it. When she told him he wrote it, he then said it was plain enough. Another characteristic of his was to dress peculiarly. I cannot describe his dress. He was always cleanly but the cut of his garments and the way he put them on was certainly peculiar. He and Judge E. L. Edwards were accustomed to traveling around the circuit together in the days when they had to make the trip on horseback. Mr. White was a very persistent man in any proposition he asserted. Judge Edwards was quick in temper and could not endure White's persistency. Once when they were about to disrobe for the night and were taking off their watches, White remarked that he always wound up his watch at night. Edwards casually remarked that he wound his up in the morning. White then proceeded to convince Edwards that at night was the better time because you had less to think about and was not so likely to forget whereas in the morning the duties of the day would have possession of the mind and one would be more likely to forget to wind up his watch. Edwards remarked that he never forgot to wind his watch and that he was in the habit of winding it then and could see no reason why he should change. White persisted in his argument contending that night was the better time. By this time Edwards had lost his patience and getting into bed said: "Wind your d__ned old watch up when you please and I will do the same." Those unpleasant incidents did not affect their friendship for no better friends ever lived.

A little further east than George White's office was the saddle and harness shop of W. D. Pratt. Besides being a saddler and harness maker he had a tanyard on the corner of Marshall and McCarty streets. He also had an ice house on High between Marshall and Lafayette streets. I don't think he delivered ice. I remember that we had to get our ice before sun-up for at that hour he closed the door and I don't think he would open it for anyone except for the sick. He was noted for his love of hunting and always had guns and dogs. He had a large family of boys and girls but I do not know what became of them. He lived to a good old age and died in this city. He was for many years an auctioneer and held sales every Saturday evening at his place of business. I have often wondered why someone did not follow that business in those days. You could take any article you did not want to keep any longer and leave it at his place and the next Saturday he would auction it off for what it would bring.

He was a man of very strong will power. A story was told of him which I have no reason to doubt. When he was a young man, he drank very hard and was in the habit of taking his jug to the saloon and getting it filled almost every day. One morning, as was his custom, he left home with his empty jug and proceeded to the saloon. When he reached the place which was on the corner of a street, he saw three other men approaching from three several directions. He knew them well and said to himself: "These three men are drinking themselves to death and in less than five years they will fill drunkard's graves." Then the thought came to him that he was drinking more than anyone of them and that the fate that awaited them would be his too. He set the jug down where he stood and went home and from that day for the forty or more years that he lived afterwards, no man ever knew of his drinking another drop of anything that would intoxicate. Just a short time before his death, he told our mutual friend Hon. P. T. Miller that he took no obligation nor did he tell anyone that he intended to quit drinking but just quit and never tasted liquor afterwards. It is refreshing in those degenerate days of so-called whiskey cures to know that there lived a man whom many of us knew that had will power to do what he wanted to do or rather quit doing what he did not want to do. I have a theory which my experience has greatly confirmed - that there are few men who cannot quit doing what they do not want to do. The trouble with the most of us is that we don't want to quit. I knew a man who quit using tobacco after thirty years constant use, sometimes chewing and smoking both at the same time. His experience was that he realized that he ought to quit and that it was destroying his nervous system and in time would give him heart disease from which he could never recover and still he did not want to quit. The struggle was to desire to quit. After he had created, by an exercise of his will power, the desire to rid himself of such a terrible habit, the victory was won and after that the sailing was comparatively easy. When the thought would come to him that never again in his life would he be allowed to enjoy the consoling influence of a delicious cigar or roll under his tongue the sweet morsel of a quid of tobacco, he wished deep down in his heart that he had never attempted to quit. The only safe whisky cure is a fixed determination not to drink and constant avoidance of the society of those who do drink. A fixed determination not to do wrong and a reliance upon yourself with faith in the assistance of God will restore any of us from our bad habits. By ourselves, to use the language of the Widow Bedot: "We are all poor critters."

R. E. Young

The following is credited to Dr. Young's series of letters by James E. Ford in *A History of Jefferson City* published by the New Day Press of Jefferson City 1938. The date of this letter's publication is unknown as Ford did not directly cite his sources. It is likely that Ford paraphrased Dr. Young as have other authors.

Merchants of olden time had little opportunity to stock up on Christmas goods. They must go to New York or Philadelphia to buy and the river being the only means of transportation, they must get their goods here before river navigation closed.

I remember how enticing were the windows of Mrs. Goodwin who kept a toy shop where Hanszens's store is today [128 E. High]. Children and negroes began counting the time about six weeks before Christmas. Toward the close of the last week, there was a great bustling about and preparing for the day. In the country, all the corn not in the shock was shucked and put away in the crib, wood was hauled to the house and enough cut and split to last over Christmas week. Fodder for the cattle [was] placed near the fence where one person could feed it every morning. Hogs were butchered, the meat salted down and the lard rendered and put away for family use or for sale. Sausage and mince meat was made, cider barrels were put in the cellar, cookies, doughnuts and cakes enough to last until New Year. Everything was to be as free from labor during that week as possible.

[This story is continued on the bottom of page 126]

DOCTOR BERRY
A BELL OVER THE DOOR ANNOUNCED HIS CUSTOMERS

THE MISSOURI STATE TRIBUNE, SATURDAY EVENING JULY 20, 1901
PAGE 1, COLUMNS 1-2

To the Editor of the State Tribune:

On the present site of the Globe clothing store [210 E. High] stood a one-story log house of two rooms. In after years it was weather-boarded and looked like a frame. In this house lived Dr. Berry. I do not know whether he ever practiced medicine in a general way or not. When I first knew him, he kept a drug store in one of the rooms of his house. There were steps leading up from the street into the drug store. There was a small bell over the door into the drug store and when you opened the out door to enter, this little bell would ring and either the Doctor or his wife would enter from the adjoining room and wait upon you. The Doctor was tall and erect - full 6 feet in height and florid in complexion. If he ever said anything more than was necessary to properly wait upon you, it was at some other time than when I was in the house. His wife was a small, demure looking lady with black hair and eyes. She was generally the one that waited on you and seemed to thoroughly understand the business of selling drugs, candies, and toilet goods of which they kept a good supply. The Doctor seemed to be studying or making something in the other room of the house into which a door opened from the drug store. When he came out in answer to the ringing of the little bell over the door, it was with an air of inquiry in his face and a manner which seemed in my boy mind to say: "Tell me quick what you want and when you get it, hurry out for I am doing something in that other room that won't wait." Oh, how I used to long for just one peep into that room but nothing on earth would have induced me to go in there alone even if I had been sure the Doctor was out. Mrs. Berry seemed fond of children and always had a kind word for them although she had none of her own. I do not remember when it was but Dr. Berry committed suicide in that room whose contents always had for me a sort of accursed place for in after years a brother of Mrs. Berry killed her and committed suicide in that same room. I was glad when the progress of the city removed it and its site is only known to those who remain from the days of its tragedies.

The next house to the east on High street, as I remember it, was a little brick office that stood on the street with a small porch in front and steps going up from the street. This was the office of Dr. J. H. Edwards. On the east side of the lot and standing back from the street was a two-story structure with a porch in front - this was in those days the residence of Dr. Edwards. The Doctor had come here from North Carolina and was the son-in-law of Mr. Campbell[*] who lived in the bottom across the river from Jefferson City. Dr. Edwards had been educated at the University of Pennsylvania and was a man of considerable force in his profession. He was known as a careful practitioner and had great success in the treatment of pneumonia, known in those days among the laity as winter fever. The calomel treatment and blood-letting were in the height of their glory at the time of which I write. Dr. Edwards was very conservative and treated more on the expectant plan than many of his contemporaries. He very early recognized pneumonia was a self-limited disease and that the best treatment was to protect the vital powers of the patient until the crisis was reached when, if there was sufficient vital power left, the patient was sure to recover. There could have been no worse treatment for pneumonia than calomel and blood-letting for both tended toward asthenic conditions and often when the patient reached the natural crisis, his physical power had been so reduced by the treatment and the disease that recovery was impossible. And in many instances, the patient succumbed before the natural crisis was reached. The science of medicine had not sufficiently advanced in Dr. Edwards' day for him to be able to describe the reasons for the faith that was in him but being a man of strong mentality, he was able to observe and apply what experience he taught. He was called by many who did not agree with him as an "old granny of a doctor" but he was a man of very even temper and what his enemies said did not disturb him. So he became known far and wide as the man who could cure pneumonia. His head was so level that the commendations of his friends for his many successes did not give him too exalted an opinion of his power. Nor did the love of money induce him to enter the field of advertising. He lived and to his death was the friend and counselor of all the afflicted

---

[*] actually Chappell

who sought his advice whether rich or poor. And as the natural end of all such men died poor.

Dr. Edwards never was, as far I knew him, in a hurry. I remember once after the Davisons had gone to Saline county to live, father got sick and sent me, a lad of 14, to tell Dr. Edwards to come and see him. My father was a very energetic man and believed in losing no time when anything was to be done and liked all such people to do the same. When he got sick, he was sicker than he or anybody else had ever been. He told me to go and tell Dr. Edwards to come and see him as quick as he could. His office was some seven or eight blocks from our house and in the same yard with his residence. I ran nearly all the way and when I found the Doctor, he was not yet out of bed. His good wife delivered the message and I returned home. When I got there, father was no better of his sickness and much more impatient than when I had left. He shouted at me: "Where is the Doctor?" When I told him, he ordered me to go after him again and to tell him and if he didn't come along with me, to go and get some other doctor. On the second visit, I found him just getting up from the table, having finished his breakfast. I told him what father said. He quickly remarked: "Is the old man that sick!" He had ordered his horse which was standing at the gate. He walked out leisurely as if nothing was urgent, mounted his horse, and proceeded to make the call. When he got there, he found father not so sick as he expected and began in his quiet way to assure him that recovery was certain and that the delay in getting the doctor was beneficial than otherwise. Father came back at him by telling him that he now understood why he had made such a reputation for curing people - he either waited until nature cured them or killed them. If cured, he claimed the victory; if killed, the case was too far gone when he had seen it. The Doctor would have been in a "bad row of stumps" if he had lived in these days of telegraphs and telephones. People are so impatient nowadays that they won't wait for you to get out of bed to answer the telephone but immediately call up some other doctor and often when you get to the patient, you find one or two doctors there and three or four more coming and it would take more than two "Philadelphia lawyers" to decide by the code of ethics who's patient it is.

Dr. Edwards was a staunch Whig in politics and would bet on his convictions as to the result of an election. My father was a Democrat and in those days would back up his judgment with his money. In the Harrison campaign they bet on the election. I think the amount was $150. Father of course lost and not having the money to pay the bet, Dr. Edwards told him if he would build him an office after a plan he would submit, he would let him off. Father agreed and the job cost him $175. So Edwards caught him "coming and going." But in those days a gentleman paid his bets although the law exempted him then as now.

R. E. Young

The following is credited to Dr. Young's series of letters by James E. Ford in *A History of Jefferson City* published by the New Day Press of Jefferson City 1938.

continued from page 122

The children and negroes were to have a good time. Something was provided for every member of the family, from master and mistress to the tiniest baby, white or black. The stockings were hung up Christmas eve night by the fireplace for Santa Claus to fill. Sometimes master got only bricks or corn shucks because he didn't need anything. "Old Mistress" provided a large bowl of egg nog for the occasion. There was generally so much eating of candies and cakes and so much drinking of cider and egg nogs that by dinner time, the Christmas dinner was liable to get cold before the guests could be assembled. But such a dinner! Turkey, venison, back bones, spare ribs, sausage, cakes galore, doughnuts, mince pies, raisins, almonds, with cider, egg nogs and Tom and Jerry to wash it all down.

On Christmas eve night the noise began, and while it ceased for a short time in the night, it was renewed with increased vigor in the morning and continued until New Year's night. Christmas ended the year's work of the hired servant while his pay continued to New Year's day. The fiddle and banjo were heard on every hand. The week was a round of parties and balls. The writer once walked home in the snow from Columbia rather than miss Christmas week at home.

The boys fired fire crackers or guns and pistols. In the space at the crossing of High and Madison streets, a huge log fire was kept going, fed by empty goods boxes and barrel staves. Around this fire all Christmas eve night and Christmas day, a motley crowd of men and boys stood firing crackers, pistols and shot guns. As the whiskey the men drank began to warm them up, the fighting began. Pistols and knives were rarely used and it was the exception if both parties did not apologize when they got sober.

W. E. DUNSCOMB
HELD THREE IMPORTANT POSITIONS AT THE CAPITOL

THE MISSOURI STATE TRIBUNE, SATURDAY EVENING JULY 27, 1901
PAGE 1, COLUMNS 1-2

To the Editor of the State Tribune:

In my last letter, the printer made me say that Dr. J. H. Edwards married a Miss Campbell. This was certainly a mistake either of mine or the printer. His first wife was a daughter of the late John Chappell and half-sister to the Hon. Phil E. Chappell now of Kansas City. The Doctor's family by his first wife consisted of four daughters and four sons. After the death of his first wife late in life, he married a lady from St. Joseph and subsequently went there to live. There were no children following this last marriage. One of his daughters married Frank M. Dixon and is now living in Texas. Her name was Margaret and she was considered one of the prettiest girls ever raised in Jefferson City. My recollection is that a Mr. Davis of St. Louis married Cam Edwards and after her death, he married her sister Alice. Cora died quite young. Thomas Edwards studied law and moved to Montana where he became quite prominent in the politics of that State. He represented one of the counties in that state. I believe [it was] the one in which Helena is situated. However, he died too young to have reached the eminence to which his ability in all probability would have lead him. John was afflicted with imperfect speech and although the doctor tried everything that promised relief, John was never able to talk plain enough for anyone except those who knew him intimately to understand him. The other two boys, Ernest and Walter, were small when their father married the second time and grew up in St. Joseph. They were never about Jefferson enough for me to remember them.

Next to Dr. Edwards' residence on High street was that of Hon. W. E. Dunscomb. I think Mr. Dunscomb was a native of New York but of this I am not certain. He came to this State before I could remember and married a daughter of Dr. Dorris, the father of Pope Dorris of whom I have spoken in these letters before. Of this union several children were born, many of them now living in this city and well-known to your readers. Mr. Dunscomb was of medium height, of light complexion, and wore a long flowing beard. He was pleasant in his manners and inclined to be reserved in his conversation. I do not know whether he was a professional lawyer or not. When I first knew him, he was employed at the capitol. He must have been a great worker or the State had much less business in those days than now. For when I first remember Mr. Dunscomb, he was clerk of the Supreme Court, chief clerk in the Auditor's office, and Commissioner of Permanent Seat of Government. He filled all these positions with credit to himself and honor to the State. He was very fond of fishing and I think he was on a fishing expedition when Peter Glover was stricken down with a disease that ended in his sudden death of which I will speak later on and correct a statement recently made in regard to this unfortunate gentleman.

Mr. Dunscomb was one of the brightest Masons in the State and filled many important positions in the grand lodge of this State including that of grand master. I think he was one of the charter members of Jefferson Lodge No. 43. If not, he was one of the early members and did much towards its building. His portrait now adorns the halls of Jefferson Lodge. He was one of the first if not the first bankers of this city. He, Thomas Miller, R. L. Jefferson, and Phil Chappell were the originators of the Exchange Bank of this city in a little brick building just north of the present "Doctor's Office." Prior to this, E. B. Cordell & Co. kept money on deposit but did not pretend to do anything like a banking business. The people had great trust and confidence in E. B. Cordell and would take any surplus money they might have and leave it with him in his big iron safe which was supposed in those days to be both fire and burglar proof. Mr. Dunscomb has been dead many years now and his esteemed widow still lives in the city and is well known to many of your readers and at no time in my life have I ever heard a disparaging word spoke of Wm. E. Dunscomb.

There were no more houses on High street after leaving the Dunscomb residence until you reached the spot now occupied by the residence[s] of Mr. [James M.] Seibert and J. R. Edwards [315 E. High]. Here was a row of two or three one-story log houses which had at one time in the history of Jefferson City been occupied by the Legislature, county court, and state treasury. When Missouri was a territory and for the first year or perhaps two after her admission to the Union, the capital was at St. Charles. And when it was established in this city, the offices were removed to the one-story log houses above described. It was rather a strange incident that in after years a State Auditor should live on the very spot of the first capitol. This property in the time of which I write was the property of the late Judge R. A. Wells who lived across the street in the building now the residence of Mr. R[udolph] Dallmeyer. I have spoke of Judge Wells before in these letters. He was, at the time of which I write, Judge of the Western district of Missouri and held his court in the old County Court house which was torn down only a few years ago.

Judge Wells' first wife was a Rector - a family originally from Kentucky. One of her brothers was one of the early governors of Arkansas. They were noted for their great courage and honorable bearing. To this union three children were born - two daughters and a son. The older daughter, Mary, became the wife of General M. M. Parsons [and] she died young after bearing two children, a son and a daughter, both of whom are now dead. The son William [Wells] I think is still living in St. Louis. By the second wife, Judge Wells had two daughters and a son. If they are living, their residence is probably in Washington, D. C. Judge Wells was a Democrat and slave owner but cast his lot with the Unionists when the war began. He was a brave man, upright judge, good neighbor, and sincere friend. On account of his quiet manner and seclusive habits, he was not popular but the few people who did succeed in breaking through his crust of reserve found him a warm-hearted companionable gentleman.

There were no more houses after leaving Judge Wells' and going east until you reached a point about opposite to where Mr. M. R. Sinks lives [515 E. High]. There in a one-story brick house with gable end towards the street lived a queer specimen of the human family. Everybody called him "Guinny Joe." He was a fair specimen of the Guinny negro and had perhaps been imported direct from Guinea, Africa. He was about 5 feet 6 inches tall and so black that charcoal would make a white mark on him. Where he came from or how he got here and how he possessed his home I never heard anyone say. But he was what we called in those days a "free nigger." All the boys of my age, white and black, were as afraid of him as it is supposed we would be of his Satanic Majesty. He had a garden back of his house and it had fruit trees in it with plenty of fruit on them in the fruit season. In the watermelon season, there were plenty in "Guinny Joe's" patch that would make your boy mouth water to look at but they were safe from the ravages of any of our "gang." I used to hear that he was very kind to the girls and would often give them of his ripe fruit and melons. Whenever he saw any of us boys about his place, white or black, he would say in his broken English: "git out you little debils," and we staid not on the order of our going. The "niggers" said he was the genuine old "hoo-doo" and if he ever threw a "yeller" powder he had on you the flesh would come off the bone wherever it touched you. I do not know what became of "Guinny Joe." When he moved to the country, I lost sight of him.

On the corner of High and Marshall streets is a frame house now standing - the last old landmark in that locality of my boyhood days. The Widow James with her mother and sisters lived in this house. Her mother and sisters were named Pulliam and they sewed for a living. Mrs. James had a son about my age named Billy. We were often together but it would not be long until we would be fighting. I think we fought every time we met but still we liked each other for the most part.

R. E. Young

OLD TANYARD

HOW LEATHER WAS TANNED YEARS AGO IN THIS CITY

THE MISSOURI STATE TRIBUNE, SATURDAY EVENING AUGUST 3, 1901
PAGE 1, COLUMNS 4-5

To the Editor of the State Tribune:

Across the street from the Pulliam residence on the corner of Marshall and High streets was the residence of W. D. Pratt of whom I have before spoken. Mr. Pratt's property extended as far south as McCarty street and on the lot fronting on McCarty and Marshall streets was located his tannery. A tannery in the days of which I write consisted of a shed under which the tan-bark was stored, a shop in which the leather was dressed and prepared for the market, a yard in which were several rows of vats with sufficient space between them for the tanner to walk in attending to the hides placed in the vats, and a circular yard around which a horse walked tramping the tan-bark to powder for use in the vats. The hides were placed in the vats in layers and the vats were then filled about two-thirds full of a liquid containing the tan-bark with perhaps some other ingredients. It took from seven to fourteen years to tan leather after this process. The tanner, besides buying hides and tanning for himself, would take hides to be tanned on shares. That is, the tanner would take a part of the leather for allowing the hide to stay in his vats. The party bringing the hide would generally take what leather he was entitled to rather than wait until the hide was tanned. They have some more rapid way of making leather now and you never see any of these old tanyards. Mr. Pratt did a thriving business with his tanyard for there was no other in the county. Some years after, there was one established at Russellville owned and operated by Mr. Peter Shackels. Both yards have long since passed away. Mr. Pratt lived in a very secluded and quiet manner and as long and as well as I knew him, I do not remember ever to have seen Mrs. Pratt.

After you left the Pratt residence going east, the next house was a one-story frame on the south side of High street where Henry Ruwart's house now stands . A Mr. John Uncopher[*] lived there. I do

---

[*] Uncapher; unclear if Henry Ruwart, Jr. or Sr., both lived in 700 block of E. High

not remember how he looked nor what he followed. I do not think I would remember there was such a man living there at that time if he had not sold my father a dapple-gray horse that was so wild father could [only] with great difficulty ride him. One day he ran away with father. He managed to keep him on the road until he came to a deep gully. By an extra effort, he managed to clear the gully and land safely on the other side. After that, he never attempted to run off again and became a very valuable horse. At this time the streets had not been graded and it was a very steep ascent up this part of High street. Most of the travel in those days turned into Main from Cherry street on account of this steep hill.

There were no more houses after leaving the Uncopher[*] residence until you reached a one-story brick house on the north side of High street near Ash street. This was the residence of Judge E. L. Edwards. Judge Edwards came to Jefferson City early in the 30's from East Tennessee. I do not know whether he was a lawyer when he came or whether he studied law in this state. He took a very prominent position at the bar and was the contemporary of Napton, Scott, Hayden, Leonard, and many others who were considered "giants" in those days. Besides being foremost in the law, he was also prominent in politics. His father,[**] John C. Edwards, was elected Governor in 1844 and Judge E. L. Edwards was attorney-general. He filled this office with credit to himself and honor to the state. He was senator of this district, member of the House of Representatives from this county, and died while on the circuit court bench of this judicial district. He was an upright man, good citizen, and just and impartial judge. My father, who knew him well and was as fond of him as he could have been of a brother, said of him when he was elected judge, that he hoped he would not have to go into Edwards' court. When asked why, he said Edwards was so upright that for fear his friendship might bias his judgment, he would be inclined to give his enemy the benefit of all doubts. Judge Edwards said in a speech once that he helped clear away the hazel brush where the City Hotel now stands. So he must have been one of the earliest settlers. He was a candidate for a seat in the convention of 1861 on the Secession ticket and was defeated by J. Proctor Knott who afterwards became a distinguished

[*] Uncapher
[**] actually brother

member of Congress from Kentucky. Judge Edwards was at all times an unswerving Democrat, one who stood on the platform of principles enunciated by his party in convention assembled and gave the ticket his active and undivided support. He did all his fighting in selecting the delegates and his arm was never puny but after the adjournment of the convention, his coat was off and his sleeves rolled up, so to speak, for the whole ticket until after the votes were honestly counted. He was no mean debater and whether at the bar or on the hustings, he was the peer of anyone he ever met in these parts. He was a methodical man in all he did and when he met his antagonist, he was sure to discover that Edwards had left no gaps down and would not fail to enter any his enemy left open. At times he was impulsive and for a short time would lose his temper. Hayden said of him once: "The only way to beat Edwards is to tease him until he loses his temper but if you ain't d___ quick to take your advantage, he will be up and at you on another tack."

When he was on the bench, he was very lenient towards members of the bar when they were out of temper. He would admonish them by calling their attention to the power of the court but seldom exercised that power against them. I heard him once, in sentencing a culprit, tell him that his offense would fully justify the court in giving him forty years but as he was a young man and could reform, he would only give him the minimum for the offense. The prisoner was angry and replied: "I don't care what you give me." But the good Judge replied: "Your angry words will not change my judgment although you richly deserve the longest time."

Judge Edwards, like all just and brave men, had a high appreciation of the gentle sex. A man arraigned before him in civil suit had been found guilty of a [text was not printed in paper - ed.] The jury had found him guilty and the Judge in approving the action of the jury, spoke at some length in a very feeling manner. Among other pointed observations upon the conduct of the young man, Judge Edwards said: "There is hardly any punishment known to the law too serious for a man who would trifle with the affections of a woman or be guilty of dishonoring her." And when he got through, everybody in the house felt that the punishment meted out by the court was richly deserved by the defendant.

EDWARD LIVINGSTON EDWARDS

At the time my father knew Judge Edwards, horse racing was very popular in and around Jefferson City. The principal race track was near the present Wardsville on the farm of Mr. Warren Dixon. Just how often they met out there for the races I do not know but among those who were nearly always present were Judge Edwards and my father. Father was married and the father of two children but Judge Edwards was single. Father soon observed that there was another attraction than the races for Judge Edwards. Uncle Warren, as he was familiarly known, had a beautiful daughter just blooming into womanhood. It was easily seen that Mr. Edwards cared more for the fair damsel than he did for the winning horse. Miss [Ann] Dixon was vivacious and could easily entertain two or three gentlemen while Judge Edwards, by no means taciturn, was inclined to be quiet in the presence of ladies. He was as brave as Julius Caesar with men but in the presence of the fair sex, he was as timid as a fawn. But after awhile, by continued effort and a suggestion from my father that a faint heart never won fair lady, he proposed and was accepted. Father used to say if Miss Ann had said to him nay, he would never have survived the wound. Several children were the result of the marriage of whom I will speak in my next.

R. E. Young

JUDGE EDWARDS
WAS THE FRIEND OF THE YOUNG MAN

THE MISSOURI STATE TRIBUNE, SATURDAY EVENING AUGUST 10, 1901
PAGE 3, COLUMNS 3-4

To the Editor of the State Tribune:

In my last letter, the printer made me say that Judge E. L. Edwards was the son of Gov. John C. Edwards. The fact is that he was the brother of Gov. Edwards. The wife of Judge Edwards was Miss Ann Dixon prior to her marriage. She was the daughter of Mr. Warren Dixon who emigrated to this State early in the 30's from North Carolina or from Virginia. I do not remember which. He was a farmer and tobacco and fine stock raiser. He was well-known in and about Jefferson City and as I said in a previous paper, had a race track somewhere on his premises near the present Wardsville. He was somewhat eccentric and there were many witty sayings of his that his friends like to repeat using the phrase "as Uncle Warren would say." One I remember was in speaking of a man that appeared to be governed largely by his wife. He would say: "The gray mare is the best horse in that team." Another was in speaking of a man who had trifling or disreputable sons-in-law: "The devil owed that man a grudge and paid him in sons-in-law." I may have occasion to speak of Mr. Warren Dixon again in these letters.

Of the children of E. L. Edwards, there are three now living in Jefferson City well-known to your readers. Of them, there is no need that I should speak at any length. They are Joseph R., John W., and Miss Sallie. William was the name of the other son. He was a very bright boy and bid fair to make a brilliant man. He was not quite old enough to go into the army with the first volunteers but in 1862 tried to join Price's army in the northern part of Arkansas. Near Rolla in Phelps county, he was wounded in an encounter with the Federals and died of his wounds.

Judge Edwards was elected to succeed George W. Miller and was twice elected to succeed himself. He was popular with the people and with the bar. He was the friend of the young attorney and many are living today who have occasion to remember his kindness and many efforts to advance them in their profession. Judge Edwards was not only kind to the young men in his own profession but was always ready with advice and recognition to help those young men he saw growing up about him. Young men in starting out in life often find it difficult to obtain the confidence of those who have known them in their childhood days and frequently have occasion to verify the proverb that a "prophet is not without honor save in his own country." The writer had known Judge Edwards from his earliest childhood days and when he began the practice of medicine in his native town, Judge Edwards was the first of those who had known him as a boy that recognized him as a physician. And it became his pleasing duty to administer to his last requirements before the cold hand of death was laid upon him.

> *We weep not for the faithful friend,*
> *Thy sleeping cannot be the end.*
> *Thy cheering voice we hear no more,*
> *But count they kindness o'er and o'er.*
> *Thy faith in God and deeds while here,*
> *Must find reward beyond thy bier.*
> *And when for us Time's sands have ran,*
> *May we like thee a crown have won,*
> *And with thee in the heavenly fields,*
> *Gather the fruit their richness yields.*

Mrs. Ann Edwards, the widow of Judge Edwards, still remains. Her years are covered with honor. None ever knew Mrs. Edwards except to love her. My father knew her well and often told me of her graces when a young lady and it has been my good fortune and pleasure to know her as the physician alone knows. Patient, affectionate, and considerate of the comfort of all about her - husband, children, neighbors, and friends. She has lived a life of usefulness and love and she can await the dreaded summons assured that there is laid up for her treasures that cannot be tarnished and of which she cannot be deprived.

In leaving High street to reach the inhabited portion of McCarty street coming west, there was a considerable waste to pass over at the time of which I am writing. The first house was a frame structure recently tore down to give place to a more imposing on the corner of

Lafayette and McCarty street. It was occupied by Mr. McDaniel Dorris. At the time I first knew Mr. Dorris, he had a distillery near where he lived. His productions of whisky and brandy were as clear as spring water and although he said they were as harmless as buttermilk, men were known to do all sorts of foolish things after freely imbibing them. And it has been said that some men engaged in trying to kill snakes which their friends who had not imbibed were unable to see. Mr. Dorris was a Master Mason in good standing to the day of his death and was buried with all the honor that order pays to any man. He was an upright man and no man ever lived in Jefferson City that was better liked than he. He was another man that thought a boy could grow up in his native town and at least be equal to the stranger that grew up God only knew where and how. He did not think it was wrong to distill and sell liquor at a fair profit provided one made "honest goods" as an old Jew friend of mine used to call good liquor. But when the "infernal revenue law" came, he quit.

There were no more houses on McCarty street until after you crossed Adams street. On the south side of McCarty near Adams, there was a one-story log house weather-boarded in after years in which Judge [H. W.] Long lived. Judge Long was for many years on the county bench and was a leading Methodist. He was a popular man and generally liked by all the people. He recently died in Saline county after a useful and upright life.

The next house on the same side of McCarty street going west was the county jail. Mr. John Duncan was the jailor. At the time about which I am writing, it was a two-story structure of stone. The jailor and his family lived downstairs and the prisoners were kept in the upper story. Mr. Duncan was jailor from my earliest recollection until the beginning of the civil war. Besides being jailor, he was also janitor at the county court house. I do not know where he came from to this State but it must have been at a very early day in the State's history. He was a jovial gentleman and ready at all times to give you advice whether it was in law, politics, or medicine. I remember once I had been suffering with what was called ague in those days. All the doctors in town and in the county, too, including an uncle doctor, had a trial at curing the ague on me without avail. One day after having a chill, I struck Mr. Duncan. He told me he would get me some Wahoo bark and I could put [it] in whisky and that a couple of tablespoonfuls of the compound taken three times daily would cure me of the chills or ague as it was called. I took the medicine and I got well of the ague. But I want to tell you that for bitter quinine isn't in it. It is not only bitter to begin with but the bitter never quits until it is time to take it again. However, it is a center shot for old time ague. Mr. Duncan was brother-in-law of B. H. McCarty and J. D. Curry and W. D. Pratt, all four marrying daughters of Mr. Hughes. I do not remember Mr. Hughes but often heard my father speak of him as a jolly, corpulent gentleman who liked a good horse. Duncan's family as I remember it consisted of two sons, Jack and Henry. Both of them went with us to the Rebel army but I do not know what became of them. In the days of Mr. Duncan, men who held minor positions of jailor and janitor were allowed to remain as long as they faithfully filled the position. In these degenerate days, in politics, men are removed no matter how insignificant the place to give room for the heeler and ward bummer who claimed to be "my friend."

R. E. Young

BOYS' TROUBLES
"DON'T CRY, BUT STRIKE BACK," SAID THE FATHER

THE MISSOURI STATE TRIBUNE, SATURDAY EVENING AUGUST 17, 1901
PAGE 1, COLUMNS 1-2

To the Editor of the State Tribune:

After leaving the jail going west, the next house was on the south side of McCarty - a frame two-story house. I don't know who lived in it at the time of which I write. Our family lived in it when I was about 6 or 7 years old before my father built the house in which Clem Ware lives. We had just moved to town from a mill on the Moreau afterwards known as Glover's mill. When my father lived there, it belonged to my Grandmother Dillinger's* estate. I had lived in town before when quite small but knew nothing of town boys' ways. I had three sisters older than myself and I had been taught not to fight and when I was imposed upon, I was in the habit of appealing to my mother who generally saw me righted. As I was the youngest child and only boy, I am at this distance inclined to think the loving mother was inclined to see my side of the argument.

One afternoon near supper time, Tenny Mathews, a boy about my age, came by our house with a large book under his arm. The book had pictures in it. He showed it to me and I became very much interested. In handling the book, I let it fall in the dirt and for my carelessness, Tenny slapped me in the face. In obedience to my peaceful teachings, I ran home crying to my mother. Father was sitting at the table and when he heard my story amidst my tears, he exclaimed: "Clear out of here, you baby. If a boy hits you, hit him back and whip him if you can and if you can't, don't come bawling to your mother about it." I never needed any more instruction along that line. The next boy that struck me got the best I had in my shop. And although I frequently got worsted, I had the satisfaction sometimes of being the victor. Since my boyhood days, I have often seen town-raised boys lord it over a country-bred youth and have always felt a kind of gratification if the town chap got licked which not infrequently happens.

---

* Dellinger's

Next to this house in which we lived was and is the McCarty House [120 E. McCarty]. I shall not attempt to describe this old-time hostelry as it existed in those days because it has been often done by more fascinating pens than mine. When I first remember the hotel, it was not more than half as long as it is today but the part toward the east is very much as it was then. The present office with its open fireplace is just the same as when the old-fashioned stage coach stopped in front of the door and the passengers from St. Louis and from the western towns alighted to enter and receive the hospitality of as two good people as ever lived in Jefferson City or anywhere else for that matter. Burr McCarty was a typical Southern gentleman and was born somewhere in Virginia. He was fond of his friends and not vindictive toward his enemies. He liked a good joke and could tell one himself. On account of his good-nature, his friends told many laughable stories of which he was the center figure. All the years I knew Mr. McCarty I never saw him angry or heard of his being in a personal difficulty of any kind but my father said he was a man of physical courage and would, if required, take care of himself.

He was passionately fond of horses and in connection with his hotel kept a livery stable. He kept the very best horses and turnouts the country could afford and imported the first "bus" ever seen in town. When we rebels left town to go to the war, one of his two-horse carriages and team with the driver was taken along. The carriage was so arranged that the cushions could be spread out and they made a nice bed. This carriage was occupied by General [M. M.] Parsons for two years of the war. He slept in it at night and if tired or indisposed, rode in it in the daytime. I do not remember the driver's name but he was a German and spoke the "sweet German accent" to perfection. I do not know whether he was a rebel when we pressed him and his team into the service or not but long before the war ended, he was as true a rebel as ever uttered the "yell."

In politics, Mr. McCarty was a "Platform Democrat" and in religion a Southern Methodist and died a consistent member of that sect. In the great Benton split in the party in this State, he was with the anti-Benton wing and was always found shoulder to shoulder with Parsons, Rogers, the two Jeffersons, Edwards, Davison, and Young in every political contest in the county and State.

Mr. McCarty was very proud of his family, especially so of his wife. Once he was passing the hotel in the presence of General G. A.

Parsons, a man of whom he was very fond, [and] after he got through, the General said: "It would be a sorry place if it wasn't for Mrs. McCarty. She keeps the house and you do the standing around." He replied: "You are right General, Alzira can't be beat keeping house and setting a good table."

Mrs. McCarty was a large women inclined to be corpulent but in her mature womanhood, she was very active and was unceasing in her efforts to make her guests comfortable. Very few who ever enjoyed her hospitality as a guest were willing to stop anywhere else when in the city. She was not only a good landlady but was also a good neighbor. If her guests or neighbors had troubles, they were hers also and nothing could ever have induced her to make use of that miserable, petulant, modern phrase: "I have troubles of my own." She had a splendid memory and I doubt if there was a child, white or black, born at the time of which I am writing in Jefferson City that the day before she died, she could not have told the day and year of their birth. She told me just a short time before her death, that she remembered my birthday well, [and] that it was on the 29th day of February during the biggest snowstorm that ever struck Jefferson City. She knew nearly all the public men of Missouri personally no matter what party they belonged to. I do not believe that Mrs. McCarty ever forgot anyone with whom she got acquainted. This made it very agreeable to those who had stopped at the hotel to stop again. She, like her husband, died a consistent member of the Methodist church. Mr. and Mrs. McCarty raised four boys and two daughters. The children have all lived here and are well-known to your readers. Miss Ella keeps the hotel just as her father and mother did and no one after stopping at the McCarty house wants to put up at any other hotel in Jefferson City.

Just below the McCarty House on Madison street close to the alley lived the Widow Dean. Her husband died before I could remember and I do not know what he followed. She was a sister of Dr. Tennessee Mathews and mother of the at one time well-known clothier and gents' furnishing goods dealer, Wm. Dean. She had a daughter named Mary who married a Mr. Yost and perhaps lives in Sedalia.

On the other end of the alley at Jefferson street in the rear of the McCarty House lived the Widow Robinson. Her husband was a carpenter and builder and a competitor of my father. He died before I could remember. She was quite a character in early Jefferson City. Everybody I ever heard speak of her said she was an excellent, motherly woman. She was one of the most rapid talkers I ever knew and never seemed at a loss for something to say. She had two daughters and one son. Jack was a steamboat pilot and was blown up on some boat in St. Louis. He left a handsome life policy in favor of his mother which made her comfortable for many years. Her oldest daughter married T. L. Crawford of the once well-known firm of Coloney, Crawford & Co.[*] - General T. L. Price being the company. Her other daughter, Bettie, married a civil engineer that came here as an employee of the Missouri Pacific railroad. They moved to Holland or Belgium where they now live. His name was Mase Gesteranus and he was said to be of noble lineage.

The character of the Robinson family was a colored boy named Sam. Many of your readers will remember him. He could punish more whisky and stand up under it better than any man, white or black, I ever knew. I used to play with Sam when we were boys and it took a good marble player to win Sam's marbles. He worked for Mrs. Robinson until Lincoln's proclamation set him free and had a good comfortable home. After he was free, he lived a sort of precocious existence. He was for a long time janitor of one of the banks and Sam's honesty was proverbial. He was also a janitor for one of the saloons. Sam always appeared to be just about so full of whisky - never staggering drunk and never entirely sober. I asked him once why he drank so much. He said the good Lord put it here among the other good things and he intended to have his share. He certainly did. But it finally served him as it never fails to serve all who drink it constantly to excess - it killed him.

R. E. Young

---

[*] Cloney, Crawford & Co.

THOMAS MILLER WINSTON

REMINISCENCES OF OLD-TIMERS

THE MISSOURI STATE TRIBUNE, SATURDAY EVENING AUGUST 31, 1901
PAGE 4, COLUMNS 3-5

To the Editor of the State Tribune:

In my writing about early Jefferson City, I have followed the leading streets through town as I remembered them and their inhabitants. In writing of the few I have not mentioned, except incidentally as I passed along, I will have to dodge about and if I miss any, it will be either because I did not know them or they escaped my memory.

On the hill just back of Friemel's Garden was a two-story house in which Robert Ainsworth and his family lived. Ainsworth was either a Scotchman or an Irishman. I do not know which. He was a stonecutter and stonemason and came here to work on the capitol in 1836 or 1837. He either built or helped to build all the early stone structures in and about Jefferson City. Not finding enough work here to keep him busy, he was in the habit of taking contracts away from here. His family, as far as I knew them, consisted of wife and two sons, Robert and William. Robert was the elder and about my age. He belonged to our "gang" and I was with him a great deal. We had many physical arguments and as we were about the same size, neither was always the victor. We were both high tempered and quick to scrap but neither held a grudge and the first time we met after a fisticuff, no one could tell that there had ever been any difference between us. The balance of the "gang" called us the "fighting Bobs." I do not know what became of the Ainsworths but if Bob is living, I would enjoy a handshake with him.

Not far from where the Ainsworth's home stood, in a two-story house, Mr. Thos. Winston lived. He was familiarly known as "Long Tom," being very tall and slenderly built. He was a druggist when I first knew him. He was a leading member of the Methodist Church, South [and] lead in the choir - that is, sat on the front seat and started the tune. Sometimes Dr. Pope Dorris was there to help him but most of the time Mr. Winston did the leading alone. He was very prominent in church work and a Sunday School teacher as well. In politics, he was a Whig and thought Henry Clay was next to perfection in statesmanship. When the fight was on in Missouri between the Democrats and Whigs, Mr. Winston was in the forefront of the conflict but in 1854 when the Whigs broke up, some going to the Republicans and some to the Union party, Mr. Winston went to the Democrats and ever after was a consistent fighting Democrat. He held several important positions in the county and state. At one time, he was commissioner of Permanent Seat of Government and at another sheriff and collector of Cole county. He raised a large family of children, all of whom are living and well-known to your readers. George Winston, our present police judge, is one of his sons. Another familiarly known as "Darb" [Benjamin] is foreman in your composing room. Mrs. Winston is still living though well stricken in years. She had always been of a retiring disposition and I do not remember when I last saw her. Thomas is an invalid and is confined to the house. He at one time in his life was deputy county clerk and my father, who at that time was the presiding judge of the county court of Cole county, often remarked that Thomas was the most efficient clerk he ever knew. The daughters are known to many of your readers and live with their widowed mother.

A little farther east on the same hill with the Winstons was the residence of George W. Miller. Judge Miller was one of the strongest characters that ever lived in Jefferson City. Just how long he was on the circuit bench of this judicial circuit I do not know. He was on the bench many years before the war. After the war, when Democrats were disfranchised on account of their sympathy for the South or on account of the participation with the rebels, Judge Miller was defeated by a man by the name of Rice. When Rice was up for a second term, we "rebs" had a show at the polls and Miller went in with a whoop. Miller died on the bench having left a record that will rank him for all time to come as one of the foremost judicial minds of the state. He came to Jefferson City in an early day. He married a daughter of Maj. Alfred Basey* and raised a family of daughters. My recollection is that there was no son in the family.

Judge Miller was regarded as the best politician in this part of the state. When a candidate and when a judge, he made it his special business to get well acquainted with every leading man in every school district of his circuit. He rode all over the circuit on horseback and

* Basye

stopped where night overtook him. Many stories were told of how he helped the women to milk and nursed the children while they got supper. Gen. Monroe Parsons used to tell a story on him that never failed to plague the Judge although he said it was one of Parsons' campaign lies. [Parsons] said one night when they were campaigning, Parsons for legislature and Miller for the judgeship, they stopped to stay all night. The good lady of the house went to get a light and while she was gone, Miller picked up a small child and kissed it and when the lady returned with the light, there stood Miller in the middle of the room kissing a "mulatto nigger baby." Parsons said the woman set him down as an abolitionist and he sure lost her husband's vote.

He was certainly one of the most energetic, industrious campaigners in the country. He was canvassing this district for judge and on a rainy afternoon about sundown, he stopped at John Berry's on the South Moreau to stay all night and have a talk with his old friend. After they had supper and Miller was feeling quite comfortable, John Berry spoke up and asked Miller what was the matter with Judge John English[*] on the Moniteau. Miller picked up his ears and wanted to know why Berry asked that question. "Why," said Berry, "he is swearing against all odds that he will not support you this time." Miller remarked that he was surprised at that as he had always regarded English[*] as one of his staunchest friends. "Well," said Berry, "he is against you this time and you know he is a power in the east end of Moniteau county and west end of Cole county." Miller thought a moment and said: "Berry, have my horse brought out. I'll just ride around and see if I can't fix it up with him some way." No amount of persuading could induce Miller to stay all night although the rain by this time had become a downpour. It was nearly thirty miles from Berry's to English's[*] and the North Moreau had to be crossed which Miller knew would be past fording by daylight. He arrived at English's about daylight and found the Judge getting up. Of course Miller told him of the all-night ride in the rain and of how distressed he was when he heard that his old-time friend was not supporting him in his present campaign. He said: "I knew there was no use in trying to sleep for if John English[*] was against me, I had just as well draw off now and save any further worry." What the difference was I never heard but suffice it to say that before Miller left, John English[*] was as

---

[*] Inglish

warm a friend as ever and supported him with his influence and vote. A great many men running for office when they hear someone is opposed to them will treat it with indifference and make up their minds to get along without that vote and its influence. Not so with Judge Miller. He would hunt the man up and try to learn from him what the matter was and if possible he would fix the matter up. If he failed, he was in as good a fix as he would have been if he had made no effort to adjust the difference. If Judge Miller knew you once, he knew you always and was just as glad to see you after he was elected as he was when a candidate. He cared nothing for money and although he secured a home, he had little left beside that when he died. He told me he began life owing Josiah Lamkin $2.50 and had never been able to get entirely out of debt from that day on to the end. He was honest and although comparatively poor, he had and enjoyed the comforts of life and left his widow enough to live on to her death.

R. E. Young

WEDDINGS IN JEFFERSON CITY
IN OLDEN TIMES

THE MISSOURI STATE TRIBUNE, SATURDAY EVENING SEPTEMBER 7, 1901
PAGE 4, COLUMNS 3-5

To the Editor of the State Tribune:

Out on Jackson street between Elm and Dunklin streets behind a two-story brick house of more modern construction stands a log house weather-boarded. Into this house more than a half-century ago, P. T. Miller took his bride Louisa Miller (nee Winston). They had only been married a few days. It was before the days of bridal tours, at least in this part of the world. There may have been a grand wedding prolonged into an infare of two or three days where the fatted calf had been slain and hundreds of friends and relatives had met and made merry with the bride and groom. In those days, it was customary to have a grand wedding at the bride's home. The day and far into the night was spent in eating and dancing and on the following day, the whole party repaired to the groom's father's house where the eating and merry-making was continued at least one day and night and sometimes for two or three days. After this, the bride and groom repaired to their own home already furnished and settled down to house-keeping and became "old folks" at once as the negroes called it. If they were wealthy, the groom took a negro-man with him, the gift of his father, and the bride took her negro maid, the gift of her father. And thus a home was at once established.

There was no such foolishness as boarding and keeping up their membership in the club. The man was voted a benedict at once and his name stricken from the list of his former companions of single men. The bride took her position among the matrons and began to learn of them what might best please her lord while the husband put forth his best energies that he might bring home a girl worthy of his wife. In spring and summer they sat on the porch or under the trees in the yard and spent their evenings in sweet converse devising means to lay stronger the foundations of a prosperous and happy home. In the fall and winter they sat by a cheerful open fire - the wife caring for the bodily comfort of her husband while he either read to her from some useful book or busied himself with mending or making some useful instrument of husbandry, casting up his accounts, or preparing himself for the labors of the following day. Now and then the married neighbors called in and spent the evening in discussing such subjects as most interested them or they called and spent the evening with a neighbor or perhaps went to assist in attending upon the sick.

It was upon such a life as this P. T. Miller and his wife Louisa entered. They never lived anywhere else. There on that sacred spot they made the battle of life together. There to them came all the joys of more than fifty years of two congenial souls made one by the law of God and man. And there came to them the sorrows incident to this unfriendly world of tears. They laughed and wept together. They on that same spot saw their children and children's children playing about their feet, saw them in thoughtless sportive youth, and saw them reach manhood and womanhood years and go forth to make alike the battle of life. There could be no happier home than that of P. T. Miller. And if sorrow came to it, they had always the consolation that it was not of their making. Thomas, as his dear wife always called him, went first. And the few remaining years of her life were spent in the fond hope that she would again see her Thomas. And when the dreaded summons came, she was wont to say: "I could bear it all if I only had Thomas here to nurse me."

> *And now, no doubt, within the pearly gates they walk,*
> *And hand in hand of all the heavenly joys they talk,*
> *It may be o'er the Jasper Walls they often lean,*
> *And view again, with glad-some hearts the old home scene.*

Mr. Miller came to Missouri from Kentucky in a very early day of the State's history. He either came with his two uncles or they followed him from Kentucky to Missouri. He was before the war a Henry Clay Whig and during the war a Union man but at all times a pro-slavery man. When the war was over, he joined the Democratic party under the leadership of the intrepid Frank P. Blair and to the day of his death was a working, fighting Democrat. In his early days, when he was a Whig, he was always ready to stand by his party. He was a consistent member of the Presbyterian Church and when they used to worship in the old stone church in the rear of the Madison

House, he was superintendent of the Sunday School and sat on the front seat and with Henry Cordell helped to "start the tune."

PHILLIP THOMAS MILLER

In his youthful days before he was married, he belonged to a coterie of youths of whom I have spoken before in these letters. They, like him, have all crossed the Silent River - Major Lusk being the last one. They were equal to any emergency when there was any fun on hand. Without exception they were in after life good citizens and useful members of the body politic. Mr. Miller was one of the first bankers in Jefferson City being connected with Wm. E. Dunscomb, Phil. Chappell, Robert Jefferson, and Alfred Morrison. For many years he was bookkeeper and confidential clerk for Coloney, Crawford & Co.* He was clerk of [the] Missouri Penitentiary for many years and afterwards Warden.

He was one of the most congenial gentlemen I ever knew. I never saw him angry in all the years I knew him but from what I heard my father say, he was a dangerous man when fully aroused. He was exceedingly fond of a joke and could tell a good story and tell it well. There never was any danger of his being interrupted when he began a story nor of anyone quitting the audience before he got through. He was known in his early days as "Little Thom. Miller" to distinguish him from his Uncle Thomas Miller who was tall and heavily built. He was a very considerate man of other people's feelings and nothing could induce him to slight or wound anyone. Soon after I graduated medicine, I met him and he in a very appropriate manner congratulated me on my advancement in life. He said: "I have always called you Bob and it is going to be difficult for me to give you your title and still I know I ought to do so. Let us compromise the matter and you allow me to call you Dr. Bob." I gave him to understand that whatever he called me would be all right as far as I was concerned. As long as he lived after that, he called me Dr. Bob.

Mr. Miller at the close of the war or soon thereafter became editor of the Tribune and made it one of the most readable papers of the time. He was an ardent supporter of T. T. Crittenden for governor and it was largely through his constant and able efforts that [Thomas] Crittenden succeeded in getting the Democratic nomination. After Mr. Miller retired from the paper, he was appointed bookkeeper in the treasury under Phil. E. Chappell. This position he held to the time of his death which occurred in the last year of Stephens' administration of that office.

While he was a captain in the Federal army and most of the time either in command of the post of Jefferson City or connected with it, he so conducted himself in office as to retain the confidence of the Federals and command the respect and good will of the rebel sympathizers. When the fortunes of war went against us and we returned to our former homes, "Little Thom." Miller met us with open arms and welcomed us to the protection his loyalty to the Union cause gave him the power to render.

---

* Cloney, Crawford & Co.

Mr. Miller raised a large family of his own besides nurtured and cared for the children of his less fortunate kinsmen. He was a man of the very highest moral attainment. And while not a total abstainer from alcoholic beverages, I never heard of his being in a saloon or being noticeably under the influence of strong drink. He was more or less connected with public life and had to do with all kinds of men and still he kept himself pure in acts and language and "by blood" was the closest anyone ever knew him to come to swearing. Several of his children are now living in Jefferson City and are well-known to your readers. George, his oldest child, is now living here with his sister Mrs. Louisa Bragg and Dr. Phil. T. Miller on the old homestead. A short time ago, his devoted wife followed him to the land of the dead having rounded out four score years of fidelity to every trust and with a never doubting faith in Him who said: "Come unto me ye that labor and are heavy laden and I will give you rest."

R. E. Young

CLONEY, CRAWFORD & CO.

HOBO HILL
THE OLD SCHOOL HOUSE OF OUR FATHERS

THE MISSOURI STATE TRIBUNE, SATURDAY EVENING SEPTEMBER 14, 1901
PAGE 6, COLUMNS 1-3

To the Editor of the State Tribune:

Just north of P. T. Miller's residence described in my last letter was a frame schoolhouse. The spot is now known as "Hobo Hill." At the time of which I write, this house was the district schoolhouse. Here, for three or four months in the year, school was held according to the school fund on hand at the time. I heard my father say that at this schoolhouse for a period of three months, I got all the free schooling any of his children got. My father was a considerable taxpayer for those days and believed in educating his children but it so happened that he always had to pay their tuition. It has been a long time since I attended school on "Hobo Hill" and it makes me sad when I think of the many happy faces that beamed on me there; too few there are left. In this town there is only one - Hon. E. L. King. There are a few others scattered here and there over the country but not many.

The teacher was a tall, slim man but well built and as strong as an ox. He had been raised and educated in this county. How much he knew and how well he was educated to teach school I do not know and I have my doubts if the directors knew. As Kipling would say, it was a good thing that we "did not know that we did not know." School teachers were hard to get in those days. They were few and far between. I have good reason to believe that all the opportunity Hazel Burlingame had to learn enough to teach the school on "Hobo Hill" was obtained at two or three terms of a three months' district school and over a tallow candle or it may have been a tallow lamp stuck in a log of the log house.

Perhaps many of your readers never saw a tallow candle. I will not attempt to describe one as they were made very much like the present star or sperm candle although made of tallow. The tallow lamp of which I speak consisted of an iron cup with a wick made of strips of cloth and filled with tallow or any other kind of grease that was handy.

At the part opposite where the wick extended in a kind of lip or tongue was the shank sharpened like a spike and three or four inches in length. This shank was stuck in one of the logs and furnished the support for the lamp. By one of these lamps or it may be by the bark thrown on the fire to make a blaze, our teacher Hazel Burlingame got most of his learning. He was an earnest, honest man and did the best he could and it may have been the best that could have been done in Cole county in those days. I remember that even such a boy as I was, I learned considerable reading, writing, and arithmetic not to mention grammar and geography. He fully convinced me that:

> *Multiplication was a vexation,*
> *Division was as bad,*
> *Care and fret, it made me sweat,*
> *Measuration ran me mad.*

Mr. Burlingame's "rules" were like those of the Medes and Persians; they varied not and the boy or girl that disobeyed them quickly found out how hard he could whip with a switch, a goodly supply of which he always kept on hand. One of his rules was that there was to be no fighting on the playground or on the way to and from school. He never inquired into the particulars of a "scrap" but whipped both parties.

I do not remember all the boys that attended school when I did. Governor Austin A. King, the Governor of Missouri, had three boys at that school, Edward, Thomas, and Austin. Austin was about my age. Ed. and Tom were older. The other boys that I remember were Geo. Roots,* Bass McHenry, Ernest Cordell, Frank and John Crandel, Jake Straus, and Nat. Hough. Some of them are living; where I do not know; more of them are dead. This was my last school in Jefferson City for after it was when my parents moved to the country and I finished my education elsewhere. There were perhaps no very great men that laid their foundations of greatness at this school but I do not now call to mind a single one now living that is not a useful member of society and those that are dead quit this world loved and honored by their fellows. No doubt there is many an "Alice" that lies under the tomb and many a "Ben Bolt" left to mourn her and sing of her graces

---

* Rootes

and beauty that was attendant at this school on "Hobo Hill" in the more than twenty years ago.

It has only been a few years since the old schoolhouse was torn down. For several years it was used for the colored school of the city. Soon after my enfranchisement and my right to participate in the government of my native city had been restored, I was a candidate for alderman in the First Ward. There was a meeting of the colored voters in the old schoolhouse on "Hobo Hill." I was anxious to get the colored vote for the whole ticket as well as for myself and consequently attended the meeting. Soon after my arrival, someone called on me to address the meeting. Speaking has at no time in my life been one of my strong suits and at this time in my life, it was perhaps my weakest point. But I was unfortunate enough to be a candidate and here the "dear people" were calling on me to declare my policy and tell them why they should support me and my party. I was totally unprepared to meet the requirements as many a poor fellow has been in the past and many a poor fellow will be in the future. But my timidity was misunderstood as was Caesar's unwillingness when he was thrice offered a crown. At last, amid the deafening calls and hurrahs for "Dr. Young," I mounted the platform and after the usual "gentlemen and fellow citizens," I proceeded to do my best which I am sure was the very poorest that could have been done.

After declaring my principles and the principles of my party, I launched out into some of the personal reasons why that collection of fellow citizens should support me. I told them that there on that particular spot I had received part of my early education and that there many of them and some of their children had received one of the greatest blessing of freedom - an education. I told them as I looked over the audience I saw many ones with whom I had played in my early boyhood days. I told them of how we had played marbles together on Sundays in back alleys and in other secluded spots, of how we had dodged our parents and gone swimming together, and of how we had slipped off Sunday afternoons and gone fishing together risking a whipping on our return, especially if we caught no fish.

Every sentence was received with a round of applause and I felt sure that I would get almost every vote in the house. Alas! for the hopes of man. Mine were destined to be soon dashed to pieces. And the time was close at hand when there would be none so low as to do the reverence. I concluded amid deafening cheers and my friends and admirers almost bore me off the stand on their shoulders. I felt happy and could almost see myself in the board of aldermen saying Mr. President, etc. I took a seat over by the door and shook hands with the "boys" within convenient reach of me.

Just then I noticed a tall, fine-looking specimen of the black *genus homo* mount the platform and wave his hand in a somewhat majestic manner. No one had called for him and no one near me seemed to know him. But his manly appearance and dignified manner seemed to command a silence of the "drop pin" variety. He had not spoken more than two sentences until I perceived he was one of nature's orators. He needed no education nor training to sway the minds of men. His powers were God-given. He told his audience that they had listened to an eloquent address and that it was very plausible. "But," he said in bassic [sic] tones that filled every crevice in the old building and made the very talker's hand tremble, "who is this former playmate of yours that so eloquently and earnestly urges you to support him? Where was he when you and your friends were struggling for that priceless liberty you now enjoy? Did he then think of you and with them enter into the great struggle in your behalf? Did he remember the childhood days he had spent with you and side by side with your friends offer his services to help set you free from the gnawing yoke of bondage? No, he spent four years of his young manhood to forge your chains stronger. He forgot his 'black mammy' to whom he so feelingly alluded [to] tonight and went forth to slay her sons and their friends in battle!"

Just then, I slid out the door and the "future proceedings interested me no more." I sneaked off down the hill and left my orator friend "alone in his glory." I was elected alderman but from that day to this I have never banked on the colored vote.

R. E. Young

THE COUNTRY
PEOPLE WHO LIVED AROUND JEFFERSON CITY

THE MISSOURI STATE TRIBUNE, SATURDAY EVENING SEPTEMBER 21, 1901
PAGE 1 COLUMNS 3-5

To the Editor of the State Tribune:

In my previous letters, I have mentioned all the people I knew in Jefferson City at the time of which I wrote. Before concluding these letters of reminiscence, I thought your readers might like to know something of the people living in the country around Jefferson City and who largely contributed to its early building and support. They were mostly from Virginia, North Carolina, Tennessee, and Kentucky. A little later, Germany furnished a large part of the early settlers.

Out on what is now known as Boggs' Hill just east of town, a Mr. Boggs lived. He was a kinsman of Gov. Lilburn Boggs, one of the earlier governors of this state. He had two sons that I knew, Henry and James. Henry's widow lives just east of the old home place on the old St. Louis road and James lives just east of her on the same road. I never knew Mr. Boggs personally but used to hear my father speak of him as a sturdy farmer and reliable Democrat. I knew both his boys and in later years we Democrats have relied largely on James to look after our interests in his "neck of the woods."

Down on the Moreau, where the St. Louis road crossed, lived a man of sterling worth, Mr. Lanson Robinson. He lived on the other side of the creek from Jefferson City and kept the ferry. Here the old St. Louis stage coach with its four or six horses, according to condition of the road at the time, crossed. In the summer, Robinson was bare-headed most of the time and bare-footed all the time. In the winter, he wore boots with his breeches stuffed in them and instead of a coat, a woolen "wampus" which his good wife made out of wool she had carded, spun into yarn, and knitted with her own hands. He was as fine a specimen of Western manhood as you could find anywhere. By his industry and frugality he accumulated quite an estate. I remember crossing his ferry one dark, rainy night in the beginning of the war when the creek was so high that he had to go quite a distance up the stream and pull the boat by the overhanging limbs of the trees skirting the banks. After we had landed on the other side and he awaited my presentation of the regular fare, I told him I was a member of the State Guard on detailed duty. He replied: "If I had known that, you damned rebel, I would have left you on the other side." I think his rough language was to throw me off my guard for I afterwards learned that he was as disloyal as I but it was more essential for him to keep his sentiments to himself than it was for me. He excited my suspicions at the time and on my return I crossed the Moreau higher up where it could be forded. Many years afterward when I became his family physician, I called up the incident and he remembered it well for soon after my night's ride, the Osage railway bridge was destroyed and he said he always connected me with its destruction.

Where the railroad bridge spans the Moreau on this side lived Robert L. Jefferson. He was a Kentuckian by birth but I do not know when he came to this state nor how old he was. He married a daughter of Judge R. A. Ewing and was a banker to this city when the war broke out. He was a rebel sympathizer and was taken to Alton [Illinois] as a prisoner of war. From there he was sent to Johnson's Island near Chicago. En route he escaped by jumping out of the car window and made his way to Kentucky. The exposure of the prison and this trip to his old home gave him inflammatory rheumatism of which he died about the close of the war. Mr. Robert Jefferson raised three daughters, Mrs. J. R. Edwards, Mrs. Charles McCarty, and Mrs. Ed. Dunscomb. All three are well-known to most of your readers.

Where the Moreau railroad bridge crossed, there was, in the days of which I write, a ferry owned and operated by Judge R. A. Ewing who lived about two miles farther east. When the railroad was seeking to cross the Moreau at this point, Judge Ewing by yielding his ferry rights obtained a contract with the railroad company by which they would forever maintain a wagon bridge at that point. The Judge was a farsighted man and before he would give the company the right-of-way through his land, it agreed to make a way station now known as Ewing's Station at which certain trains each way daily could be flagged to stop.

He was on the county bench when the Missouri Pacific railroad [was] built through this county. It sought to make this county pay a bonus to the road for the benefit the road would be to the county. The Judge knew full well there was no reasonable way around the county and so they never got a cent while Moniteau county paid them two hundred thousand dollars to go through California. I have heard it said that the road that for awhile branched from here in this county had given a bonus to the main line. It is a mistake. Judge Ewing would have been in favor of a bonus if any such condition had been proposed to him. The southwest branch, as the Atlantic and Pacific was then called, as the main line was to run through Jefferson City.

Judge Robert A. Ewing was for many years on the county bench and her financial standing today is largely due to his efforts and the sound lessons he taught. He was a Whig in politics but could always be elected judge of the county court notwithstanding Cole was a Democratic county in those days. I remember the first time my father ran for judge. Judge R. A. Ewing was also a candidate. There were three to be elected. Young, Fowler, and Ewing were elected - two Democrats and Ewing the Whig.

Judge Ewing raised a large family. Two of his sons are now living in this city. Hon. H. Clay and Hon. Ashley Ewing. They have both been honored with a seat in the lower house of the legislature. Clay Ewing, as he is familiarly know, has been Attorney-General of the state, served on the supreme court commission, and held other positions of honor and trust. Judge Ewing had three other sons, now dead, Robert, Ephriam, and Gilson. There were several daughters, Mrs. Mariah Long is the only one living. She is well-known to all our citizens.

His wife was the daughter of Mr. [Jonathan] Ramsey and lived to the ripe age of 83 years. She was a very strong character and was a great help to the people settled around her. Many of them were Germans and unaccustomed to the usages of the new Western world in which they had cast their lot. She was very popular in her neighborhood and revered after death came. Judge Ewing was sincerely mourned and her memory started and helped to maintain a school in his district and many of our citizens in and about Jefferson City were benefited by the early and constant school that was maintained in his district in those early days. The sixteenth section which was set apart for school purposes in the organization of this state in his district was very valuable and was a great help in the support of a school there.

Just below where Judge Ewing lived at the mouth of the Osage River, there was a family living at the time of which I write named Glenn. I only remember them as a family that one of my sisters visited. The house was a large two-story log house and was built just at the end of the bluff. I think there was a steamboat landing at this point and a wharf-house where boats transferred freight to smaller craft going up the Osage. There were several families living along the Osage as far up as Lisletown and Shipley's ferry but I never knew any of them except the Waltons who lived on the hill just south of Osage City of today.

R. E. Young

The following is credited to Dr. Young's series of letters by Dr. Joseph S. Summers in *Medical Milestones in Cole County, Missouri* published by Summers Publishing of Jefferson City in 1988. The exact date of this letter's publication is unknown as Summer's only cited it as an article from 1901 and titled "Jefferson City Fifty Years Ago." It is likely that Summers paraphrased Dr. Young as have other authors. According to Dr. Summers, this is in reference to Dr. Alexander M. Davison.

...a graduate of the University of Pennsylvania in medicine, he had no patience with any doctor who did not subscribe to the code of medical ethics... I used to like to go to his office for he was fond of and kind to children. He kept his own medicine and would give you a stick of licorice every time you came. He had a skeleton in his back office in a closet and all he had to do to us mischievous boys to get rid of us was to point in that direction... No night was too dark or inclement for him to ride any distance to see the sick or his suffering fellow man... During the epidemic of cholera in 1849, there were days and days that he never took off his clothes at night and many times would snatch a few hours sleep in his stable loft.

Affectionately,
*R. E. Young**

---

* From a letter to his nephew, Frederick Young Murphy, dated December 4, 1900.
  Electronically digitized by David R. Carter.

OTHER ARTICLES

CONCERNING

DR. R. E. YOUNG

THE ASYLUM OFFICERS
DR. R. E. YOUNG OF JEFFERSON CITY
CHOSEN AS SUPERINTENDENT

THE DAILY MAIL, NEVADA, MISSOURI, TUESDAY AFTERNOON JUNE 28, 1887
PAGE 1 , COLUMN 4

The Board of Asylum managers protracted its meeting yesterday evening until six o'clock when an adjournment was taken until 9 o'clock this morning.   D. C. Kennedy, who was absent yesterday, arrived this morning and the full board went into session at the appointed hour.

After a further consideration of the applications, Dr. R. E. Young of Jefferson City; Dr. B. A. Barrett of Springfield; Dr. E. J. Warth of Nevada;   Dr. Busse of St. Joseph and Dr. Hart of Brownsville were placed in nomination for Superintendent. On a vote being taken, Dr. Young was elected.

For Treasurer, W. P. Munro of Chillicothe; J. J. Tucker of Arrow Rock and W. I. Fisher of Nevada were balloted on and the vote resulted in election of Mr. Munro.

For Steward, A. Cummins, Harvey W. Isbell, and Samuel Crockett were contestants but on a count of the vote, Mr. Cummins was declared duly elected.

About fifteen physicians made application for the positions of assistants there being two to elect. The ballot resulted in an election of Dr. Gordon of Columbia and Dr. Geo. P. True of Deepwater, Henry County.

The physicians who applied for the several positions all applied with diplomas and substantial recommendations.

The matter of the election of a third assistant physician was laid over until the next meeting of the Board.

The Board of Managers is in session this afternoon considering the adoption of by-laws governing the institution.

BRIEF BIOGRAPHIES
SHORT SKETCHES OF THE LIVES OF THE
PRINCIPAL OFFICERS OF NEVADA ASYLUM

THE DAILY MAIL, WEDNESDAY AFTERNOON JUNE 29, 1887
PAGE 1 , COLUMN 4

Dr. Robert Emmet Young, who was elected Superintendent of the Nevada Asylum, was born in Jefferson City, Mo., February 29, 1840. He resided on a farm during his boyhood and was educated at the State University in Columbia, Mo. [He] served as a private in Col. Robert McCulloch's [cavalry] regiment, C. S. A., and later in Lesueur's Light Battery. After the war, he taught school in Louisiana and then returned to Cole County where he engaged in farming for three years. [He] graduated in medicine and surgery in Philadelphia at [the] University of Pennsylvania and began the practice of medicine in Jefferson City in 1871. [He] was appointed physician to the Missouri penitentiary in 1873-4 by Gov. Woodson and afterwards engaged in general practice in Jefferson City. He was appointed Commissioner for Asylum No. 3, after its location at Nevada, to fill a vacancy caused by the death of Dr. T. R. H. Smith. He is a warm personal friend and medical adviser of Gov. Marmaduke. He has a wife and several children and is a member of the M. E. Church, South. Dr. Young will move his family to Nevada at once and take charge of the work assigned to him. He stands high in his profession and is an admirable man for the office to which he has been elected.

[The other biographies have been omitted for this book - ed.]

TWO FORMER JEFFERSONIANS

JEFFERSON CITY WEEKLY TRIBUNE, JANUARY 11, 1888
PAGE 2 , COLUMN 2

In a recent issue of the Kansas City Real Estate Index, we find the following concerning two residents of Nevada but formerly of Jefferson City.

Dr. Robert E. Young was born in Jefferson City, Mo. in 1840. He was raised on a farm and educated at the State University at Columbia. He afterwards graduated in medicine at the University of Pennsylvania and practiced medicine in his native city for sixteen years. During Governor Woodson's administration, he was appointed physician of the Missouri penitentiary, in which capacity he served for two years. Dr. Young assumed his official duties upon the opening of the asylum October 1 of the present year. He is a courteous gentleman and a fine physician [and] well qualified for the high position he is filling.

Mr. B. F. Stewart located in Nevada five years ago, coming from Jefferson City. During his twelve years residence at Jefferson City, he filled the following positions of honor. He was first clerk in the state treasurer's office, was for six years clerk in the state auditor's office, and also served as clerk for the warden of the penitentiary. He was afterward appointed secretary of the state board of equalization by the governor, which position he resigned upon removing to Nevada. During his residence in Vernon County, he has held the position of deputy circuit clerk and deputy recorder of deeds and is at present serving as deputy sheriff, which position he has held since 1884. Mr. Stewart is a thorough business man, a pleasant gentleman, and an efficient officer.

COLE COUNTY POOR FARM
DR. R. E. YOUNG, MEMBER OF THE STATE BOARD OF CHARITIES AND CORRECTIONS, FINDS IT IN FINE CONDITION

JEFFERSON CITY DAILY TRIBUNE, OCTOBER 7, 1897
PAGE 4 , COLUMN 4

Editor Tribune:
    Last Sunday was a beautiful autumn day, just such a one as created a strong desire for a visit to the country. I had some charitable work to do and concluding that the better the day the better the deed, I at once gratified my desire for a ride in the country and at the same time performed my duty to the State by visiting the Cole County poor farm near Elston. I arrived at the farm near 12 in the morning and was cordially invited by the superintendent, Mr. Joseph Gibbler,* to make a thorough investigation of the farm and its inmates.
    I found Mr. Gibbler* and his wife all that could be desired in people to have charge of such an institution as a county farm. These institutions are generally called poor houses in the sense of being to shelter poor people.
    The house itself is of brick and one-story in height. The rooms are large and only one person occupies a room. They are comfortable in both summer and winter. Each room is furnished with an iron bedstead and wire-woven mattress, chair, and table - quite as comfortable as the average room in our insane asylums, since they have been viewing with each other as to how much of an appropriation they could turn back into the treasury. One of the buildings is built to house both males and females but a strong door separates them, which the superintendent assured me was kept closed at night and also in the day when neither he nor his wife were able to look after it. Still I think the county should provide a better way to keep the sexes apart. Besides this brick building, there is another house for males - a log house. This is furnished like the brick house and looks like it would be quite warm in winter by the aid of the large stove in the center of

---

* Gibler

the hall. All the rooms in both houses open on a hall extending the length of the buildings and the stoves are in the center of the halls. If fires are kept in the stoves in winter, the inmates will be kept warm and no one could doubt after an acquaintance with Mr. and Mrs. Gibbler,* that fire would be kept in the stoves.

The inmates were plainly but well dressed - better dressed than the average inmates of our asylums. It was Sunday and the inmates had free access to the grounds. Two or three of the men came in from the fields while I was there and said they had been nutting and from their hands, I judge they were telling the truth.

The superintendent told me that all the inmates did something toward their own maintenance. Those able to work in the fields were required to do so, while those who were crippled or feeble worked in the garden or about the ground.

There are three insane persons on the farm, two men and one woman. These are classified in psychology as demented and are as well cared for as such people are in the Missouri insane asylum.

The cooking is done in a kitchen common to the household, including the superintendent's family. The food is wholesome and plain and all agree they get plenty of it. The inmates looked well cared for and while I hope I may never have to dwell on a county farm, still if it must be so, I would prefer it on the Cole County farm and that Mr. and Mrs. Gibbler* be in charge.

There are some things I wish the county court could change. There are four children on the farm, two girls and two boys - the oldest, a boy eight or ten years of age, and the youngest, a baby at the breast. In the name of humanity, this ought not to be. These children, for the sake of future generations, ought not to be brought up in such an atmosphere. It is not my province to dictate nor suggest but surely a court as intelligent as that of Cole county can provide better for these children than to bring them up on the county farm. I know the taxpayers will not object to footing the bill. One other is to build a new house for the males and separate it from the present one which can be taken for females. The reason will suggest itself to everyone.

There is 150 acres in cultivation. The land is fair but nothing to be proud of. Some court in the past sold off forty acres of the best land; just why, no one seems to know.

---

* Gibler

Many of the inmates complained of nothing to read.   Papers and periodicals would be highly appreciated.

There are twenty inmates now on the farm, seven males and thirteen females. I would call them a fairly happy family. Several of them I have known for many years and they are better off now, as far as comforts go, than when they were in homes of their own.   The county court is entitled to praise for its efforts toward these unfortunate citizens.

R. E. Young

Dr. Young as a Soldier

Jefferson City Daily Tribune, August 2, 1898
Page 4 , Column 4

Series 1, volume 53 of "The War of the Rebellion" contains and official report of Gen. M. M. Parsons, showing the part taken by the Sixth division of the Missouri State Guard in the battle of Wilson's Creek.

Among other things, the report makes mention of our esteemed fellow citizen, Dr. R. E. Young, in the following manner:

"My orderly, a lad, Robert E. Young, had his horse killed under him early in the day on the field near by me. He then found a musket and fought with Capt. Champion's company during the balance of the conflict.   His coolness and perseverance were highly commendable."

DEATH OF DR. YOUNG
PASSED AWAY AT HIS HOME EARLY FRIDAY MORNING

THE MISSOURI STATE TRIBUNE, SATURDAY MORNING JANUARY 9, 1904
PAGE 1, COLUMNS 1-3

Dr. R. E. Young of this city, for years a practicing physician and one of the best known men in Central Missouri, died at his home on East Main street, a few minutes past 5 o'clock Friday morning after a brief illness. His death was sudden to his family and his great circle of friends, who were not prepared for his immediate taking off, although it was known for several days past that his chances for recovery were slight. He was conscious to almost the last.

Dr. Young has been a familiar and prominent figure in Jefferson City for a half century, being born and reared in the capital of Missouri. From boyhood his life has been an active one and he bore his age well until a year or so ago, when he began to decline and for the past few months indications of feebleness had been apparent. The immediate cause of his death was stomach trouble and weak heart action.

Few men knew more about the history of Jefferson City and its people than did Dr. Young and he loved to sit and talk of the old characters of the city and incidents of the town which have now passed into history. In addition to being an entertaining talker, he was also a good writer and contributed frequently to the columns of the local press. He had a high conception of duty and followed the dictates of his own conscience at all times. His death is sincerely regretted by every citizen who knew him and his passing away is a distinct loss to the community.

Dr. Robert Emmet Young was a son of the late Judge William C. Young of this city and was born here on the 29th of February 1840. He spent his boyhood in and around Jefferson City and when old enough was sent to Columbia to attend the State University. Before graduating at that institution the civil war broke out and Dr. Young left school a junior to follow the fortunes of the South.

He was 18 [21] years of age when he joined the battalion of Gen. Parsons and was made an orderly. Not long after he became a member of Capt. A. A. Lesueur's Battery and before the struggle was over he joined a Louisiana company, remaining with it until the war closed. He taught school for a few months and then returned to Jefferson City, where he resided for three years, when he concluded to take a course of medicine at the University of Pennsylvania, which he accomplished, graduating well up in his class. He returned to Cole county to practice his profession and secured the appointment of prison physician under the Silas Woodson administration but gave this up later to engage in active practice in Jefferson City. He enjoyed a lucrative practice and was one of the most prominent physicians in the central district of the State. He was appointed physician and surgeon of the Missouri Pacific railway and acted in that capacity. He left Jefferson City and went to Nevada [Mo], where he remained several years as superintendent of the Nevada Insane asylum. He left the asylum in 1893 and returned to Jefferson City to engage in practice again and has remained here since. Under the Stephens' administration, Dr. Young was a member of the State Board of Charities and Corrections. He was also a member of the State Medical Society and president of the Cole County Medical Society.

On the 21st of May, 1873, Dr. Young was married to Miss Charlotte McKennan* of Baltimore, Md. Two sons were born of this union, Dr. William C. Young and James McKennan* Young, well known young men in Jefferson City. Dr. Young was a Mason and a member of the A. O. U. W. lodge of this city. He was also vice-president of the First National Bank of Jefferson City.

The funeral services will be conducted Sunday afternoon at 3 o'clock by Rev. C. E. Patillo under the auspices of Jefferson Lodge No. 43, A. F. and A. M.

---

* McKenna

DR. R. E. YOUNG HAS PASSED AWAY

SOUTHWESTERN MAIL, NEVADA, MISSOURI, FRIDAY JANUARY 15, 1904
PAGE 3 , COLUMN 2

Joe Harper received a telegram, dated at Jefferson City Friday and signed by Dr. Wm. Young, which conveyed the sad intelligence of the passing away of Dr. R. E. Young, a gentleman who was well and favorably known to many of the MAIL's readers. The message says:

"Father died this morning at 5:15. Funeral Sunday afternoon."

Dr. Young was appointed superintendent of the Nevada State Insane Asylum at its opening, during the administration of Gov. Marmaduke. He came here with his family from Jefferson City where he had resided all his life, and had occupied the position of physician to Gov. Marmaduke. He served as superintendent of our asylum through the administrations [of] Gov. Marmaduke and Gov. Francis, relinquishing the position to Dr. J. F. Robinson soon after the inauguration of Gov. Stone.

While here, Dr. Young made many friends and all of our people will regret to learn of his death. He was a member of the M. E. Church, south, and was prominent in Masonic, medical, and social circles. He also took a leading part in local politics, having served as chairman of the Cole County Democratic Committee.

He leaves a wife and two sons, Dr. Wm. Young who is in the practice of dentistry at Jefferson City and James Young who is engaged in the grocery business at that place.

He was 65 [63] years old.

The MAIL extends sympathy to the bereaved family.

THE DEATH OF DR. YOUNG

THE MISSOURI STATE TRIBUNE, SATURDAY MORNING JANUARY 9, 1904
PAGE 2 , COLUMNS 1

The sad news of the death of Dr. Robert E. Young cast a shadow over the city. While only a week ago he was around town mingling in his familiar way with friends, today he goes to the great beyond, whither so many have lately been called from our midst. At last his jovial friendly smile is missed, his message of sunshine is ended, he will evermore be absent in the flesh but present in the lasting influence of a warm knit character.

The doctor was a rare type of the frank and open man, candid almost to a fault. Whatever enemies he made came from nothing less than the exercise of that inborn disposition to be open and above board with everybody and to tell the plain unvarnished truth. He had about him not the slightest self-concealment. He was just as quick to admit his own shortcomings as he was to tell a patient the facts, when facts most unwelcome.

He possessed a tender heart, and nothing pained him more than to witness the suffering of those who came under his medical care. His patients loved him, believed in him and they became almost as near to him as the members of his own family. Professionally, he was an eminent success. He had been in his earlier years the personal physician of Governors and State officials and in many cases the ties between the doctor and these men were the very strongest, notably so in the cases of Governor John S. Marmaduke, Judge John A. Hockaday, and others.

To the writer, Dr. Young had been a constant friend. Many times his advice had been sought on questions of importance. He had been true amid some trying circumstances, when true friends were none too plentiful. A personal knowledge revealed in him the soul of honor and the very keenest sense of gratitude. His life was on of good cheer. He lived on a high plain. He loved his family and his God. The love and admiration for his wife never lost any of the romance of boy and girlhood days. His life was well ordered, loyal, genuine. May his good influence be forever felt in this town and State.

Author Unknown

IN MEMORY OF DR. YOUNG
DIRECTORS OF FIRST NATIONAL BANK TESTIFY TO HIS STERLING WORTH IN APPROPRIATE RESOLUTIONS

THE MISSOURI STATE TRIBUNE, SATURDAY EVENING JANUARY 10, 1904
PAGE 4, COLUMN 3

At a meeting of the Board of Directors of the First National Bank held on the 9th instant, the following action was had:

Whereas, Death has again visited our number and has called from active service in our midst our esteemed vice-President Dr. Robert E. Young and

Whereas, by the removal of the faithful official this bank has lost the efficient and competent service of a director ever ready to perform the duties devolving upon him to the best interest of this bank without fear or favor.

Resolved, that we here record our high esteem and regard for the memory of our co-laborer and our regret that he is no longer with us for advice and counsel; that his faithfulness and integrity and earnestness of purpose has ever been of record and further

Resolved, that our sympathy be extended to his bereaved family and as a further mark of esteem the officers and directors of the bank attend the funeral services in a body.

To Attend in a Body
All Physicians of the City to Honor Departed President

The Missouri State Tribune, Saturday Evening January 10, 1904
Page 4, column 3

The Cole County Medical Society met in called meeting at the court house at 3 p.m. Saturday. Dr. Thorpe called the meeting to order.

When this society was organized a few months ago, it elected Dr. R. E. Young its first president by acclamation, recognizing in him the man well worthy of the honor and feeling that his election would reflect honor upon the society.

All the members of the society living in town being present, it was resolved to attend the funeral of Dr. Young in a body.

Drs. Hough, I. N. Enloe, and Clark were appointed a committee to draft resolutions of respect and report at a meeting to be held Wednesday next.

Funeral of Dr. Young
Services Will be Conducted at Three O'clock This Afternoon.

The funeral services over the remains of the late Dr. Robert E. Young will be held this afternoon at the residence in East Main street at 3 o'clock. The services at the house will be conducted by Rev. C. E. Patillo of the Methodist church, of which the deceased was a member. The funeral will be conducted under the auspices of the Masonic order, Jefferson Lodge No. 43, A. F. and A. M. The members of the Prince of Peace Commandery will act as escort to the grave. The honorary pallbearers selected for the occasion are as follows: Major V. M. Hobbs, Henry Ruwart, Sr., Oscar G. Burch, George B. Carstarphen, Hugh Stephens, and Charles E. Dewey.

IN MEMORY OF DR. YOUNG.

THE MISSOURI STATE TRIBUNE, TUESDAY JANUARY 12, 1904
PAGE 4, COLUMN 1

United Confederate Veterans - Headquarters Gen. M. M. Parsons Camp No. 718, U. C. V., Jefferson City, Mo., January 10, 1904.

At a meeting of this camp, No. 718, U. C. V., held on above date, the following resolutions were adopted:

Whereas, Dr. Robert E. Young, one of the charter members of this camp and an honored and exemplary Confederate soldier, than which no higher title for sterling manhood was ever bestowed, departed this life on Friday, January 8, 1904, thereby depriving this camp one of its most honored members, and the State of one of its best citizens; therefore be it:

Resolved, that in the death of our esteemed comrade and brother-at-arms, this camp has sustained an irreparable loss, a comrade who was ever loyal and devoted to the South, one who risked his life and enthusiastically gave his services to the cause he religiously believed to be right and just, and who since armed strife has ceased has given of his means to the relief of the needy and always maintained the highest standard of manhood.

Resolved that the high praise then bestowed upon him by Gen. M. M. Parsons, in his official report of the battle of Wilson's Creek, August 10, 1861, saying: "My orderly, a lad, Robert E. Young, had his horse killed under him early in the day on the field near by me. He then found a musket and fought with Captain Champion's company during the balance of the conflict. His coolness and perseverance were highly commendable." was well deserved at the time and his subsequent career showed the high encomium was not misplaced.

Resolved, that this camp will attend the funeral in a body, as our last mark of esteem and respect for our departed comrade.

Resolved that his widow and children have our heartfelt sympathy in this their saddest hour, when camp, municipality, and State each has been so badly bereft and to them we extend our sincerest condolence in their great bereavement.

Resolved, that a copy of these resolutions be spread at large upon the records of this camp and that a duly attested copy be furnished the family of our esteemed comrade.

Resolved further that a copy of these resolutions be furnish to the newspapers of Jefferson City.

JAS. B. GANTT,
Captain Commander.
THOMAS O. TOWLES,
Adjutant.

PRIVATE ROBERT "BOB" E. YOUNG
THIRD MISSOURI BATTERY, C. S. A.

LOVED DR. YOUNG
HIS WORK AT THE NEVADA ASYLUM IS A MONUMENT TO HIS MEMORY

THE MISSOURI STATE TRIBUNE, TUESDAY JANUARY 12, 1904
PAGE 4 , COLUMN 4

Harry C. Moore, in speaking of Dr. Young's death, said that he was on the asylum board eight years while Dr. Young was superintendent. That he was one of the best men he ever knew; an ideal superintendent, not only an organizer but a sympathetic, kind hearted gentleman and always a true friend. He was never narrow in his views but was built upon broad lines. He was a worker and doer of things, he took great interest not only in all the patients and employees but in beautifying the grounds. He believed in improvements. He loved the trees and flowers, the walks, fountains, and driveways. His great ambition was to make the surroundings of Asylum No. 3 the loveliest in Missouri. Marmaduke Park, adjoining the asylum, was his special pride. He wanted it to grow in beauty, not only as a monument to that splendid man and Governor, for whom it was named, but that it might be forever a place of beauty, comfort, rest, and pleasure for the patients in the years to come. **Nevada Post**

FUNERAL OF DR. R. E. YOUNG

THE MISSOURI STATE TRIBUNE, TUESDAY JANUARY 12, 1904
PAGE 1, COLUMN 6

The funeral of Dr. R. E. Young took place from the family residence on Main street at 3 o'clock Sunday afternoon. The services at the residence were conducted by Dr. C. E. Patillo of the Methodist church of which the deceased was a member, assisted by Dr. J. F. Hendy of the Presbyterian church. The remains were escorted to the Woodland cemetery by the members of Jefferson Lodge No. 43, A. F. and A. M. with the members of Prince of Peace Commandery No. 29 as escort and by the members of the A. O. U. W. Lodge, all of which lodges the deceased was an honored an highly respected member and the services at the cemetery were conducted by the Masonic lodge in accordance with the beautiful funeral rites of the order. The directors of the First National Bank and the members of the Cole County Medical Society attended in a body and paid their last tribute of respect to their deceased member and co-laborer. The day was a very disagreeable one, yet the attendance of the different societies and of the esteem in which the deceased was deed, which was another evidence of the esteem in which the deceased was held by the people of Jefferson City. The floral offerings were many beautiful ones.

THE SOUTHERN CROSS OF HONOR

THE MISSOURI STATE TRIBUNE, SATURDAY EVENING JANUARY 16, 1904
PAGE 2, COLUMN 3

Next Tuesday night at 8 o'clock at the Methodist church in this city there will be an impressive and unique ceremony.

At that time the Winnie Davis Chapter of the United Daughters of the Confederacy will present to 19 old Confederate soldiers of Gen. M. M. Parsons Camp of Confederate Veterans each "A Southern Cross of Honor." As this is the first time this has ever been done in Jefferson City, doubtless many of our readers would like to know what is meant by "The Southern Cross of Honor." The idea of conferring some emblem upon the Southern soldier who had borne himself bravely and honorably in the war between the states from 1861 to 1865 was conceived by Mrs. Mary Ann Cobb Erwin of Athens, Ga. The design offered by Mrs. S. E. Gabbett of Atlanta, Ga., was accepted by the national convention of the United Daughters of the Confederacy at Richmond, Va., in November 1899. Rules were formulated for the conferring of these badges of honor. These crosses are bestowed on June 3 of each year, the birthday of President Jefferson Davis, and on January 19, the birthday of Gen. Robert E. Lee. No veteran shall receive more than one cross but if he has the misfortune to lose it he may obtain a copy of the certificate on file and the name of the president who gave it. The cross cannot be worn except by the veteran upon whom it is bestowed. The cross itself is made out of Confederate cannons purchased by the Daughters of the Confederacy from the United States and is furnished only on certificates of eligibility, showing the enlistment of the soldier, his company, battery or other service, his brigade, his wounds, if any, and his discharge for honor or his parole on the surrender of the army to which he belonged. Great care is taken to verify these and the Confederate soldier who receives one justly prizes it as a distinguished honor. Though he lost the battle, he cherishes as his richest legacy this testimonial of the women of the Southland to his devotion, suffering, and privation in the cause of the South and every right-thinking man and woman, North and South, will rejoice with him in this soldier's pride. The cross itself is of copper and brass and is taken from the most beautiful cross in the world which lay upon the breast of Queen Dagmar of Denmark when her sarcophagus was opened after 600 years. The daughters have adopted the words of the "Darling Queen:"

> *Gifts of precious stones are not for me;*
> *Better far are noble deeds and holy*
> *Than a mighty kingdom held in fee.*

The reverse of the cross is the Confederate battle flag, the Southern cross with thirteen stars.

An exceedingly sad feature is that two of the most deserving of M. M. Parsons Camp, Dr. R. E. Young and B. F. Clark, have both died after their eligibility had been settled and their crosses ordered and forwarded to the chapter and before the day of presentation.

Just prior to the presentation of the crosses, Miss Edmonda Nickerson of Warrensburg will deliver an address. The people of Jefferson City have rarely had the opportunity of listening to a more gifted and eloquent speaker than will be afforded them in hearing this truly eloquent, but withal, modest young Missouri woman.

No one can afford to neglect this unusual treat.

The citizens of the capital city are all invited to come and enjoy these exercises.

In addition to Miss Nickerson's address and the presentation of the crosses to the old soldiers, there will be at least one other feature which everyone will appreciate.

After the exercises, the ladies of Winnie Davis Chapter and their families and the veterans of M. M. Parsons Camp, are invited to an informal reception at the home of Judge and Mrs. J. B. Gantt to meet Mrs. Gielow and Miss Nickerson.

IN MEMORY OF
ROBERT EMMET YOUNG, M. D.

THE MISSOURI STATE TRIBUNE, SATURDAY EVENING JANUARY 16, 1904
PAGE 1 , COLUMN 5

Whereas, it has pleased God to remove from our midst our friend and associate, Dr. Robert Emmet Young:

Resolved, in the death of Dr. Robert Emmet Young, the Cole County Medical Society has lost an earnest and active member and a valued officer, the medical profession one of its most charitable, kind-hearted and honorable representatives and the community a worthy, generous-minded and public spirited citizen. All classes in this city join in regretting his untimely passing to the great beyond.

Resolved, that we tender our sincere sympathy to the bereaved family and that a copy of the resolutions be sent to the secretary of the Missouri State Medical Association and that they be spread upon the minutes of this society.

CHAS. P. HOUGH,
W. A. CLARK,
I. N. ENLOE,
Committee.

WILL OF DR. YOUNG

THE MISSOURI STATE TRIBUNE, SATURDAY EVENING JANUARY 23, 1904
PAGE 2 , COLUMN 4

The will of the late Dr. R. E. Young was admitted to probate Friday and Mrs. Catherine* Young and William C. Young and James M. Young qualified as executors of it by appointment of Judge Fowler, under the provisions of the will.

Dr. Young was quite wealthy and left considerable real and personal property.

He bequeathed all his real property to his wife, Mrs. Catherine* Young, during her life or widowhood. In the event she marries, then the real property is to be divided equally between her and the sons, William C. and James M. Young.

All the bank stock of the First National Bank is given to the widow, as is the household and kitchen goods.

James M. Young is given $500 and the will requests that the office furniture and fixtures of the office of Dr. Young on High street be sold and the property divided equally between the two sons and the widow. All other personal property is to be equally divided in the same way between these heirs. After the death of Mrs. Young, then the real property is to go to the two sons.

---

* Charlotte

In Memoriam

THE MISSOURI STATE TRIBUNE, JANUARY 27, 1904
PAGE 2 , COLUMN 4

Dr. Robert E. Young, a member of Prince of Peace Commandery No. 29, Knights Templar, departed this life on Friday, January 8, 1904, aged 63 years.

Sir Knight Young, in all relations of life, was a manly man. He was a kind husband and father, a faithful friend, a generous foe.

He was a exemplary and useful citizen; always ready to assist in every laudable work. He was a man of strong convictions and tenacious of his beliefs but just in his treatment and charitable in his judgment of others.

In the death of Sir Knight Young, his family has sustained an irreparable loss; this commandery loses a worthy and highly esteemed member and the community an honored and useful citizen, who throughout life was identified with its growth and prosperity.

As a Christian, our departed frater measured up to the highest standard of Knightly honor. We mourn for him, not as those who have no hope, but with a firm belief that he will receive the reward promised by the great Captain of our salvation to those who conquer in his name.

To the bereaved family, we extend our heartfelt sympathy in their sore affliction and mingle our sorrows with theirs in our common loss.

As a further mark of our esteem, let this memorial be entered at length in our journal, published in each newspaper of the city, and a duly engrossed and authenticated copy furnished to the family of our deceased frater.

Done by order of the commandery.

H. A. GASS,
JESSE W. HENRY,
FRED H. BINDER,
Committee.

APPENDIX A

~

MAP OF THE
CITY OF JEFFERSON
1849

~

SOURCE: REDRAWN BY M. HUNTER, 1979.
COURTESY OF THE MISSOURI STATE ARCHIVES.
ELECTRONICALLY DIGITIZED BY DAVID R. CARTER.

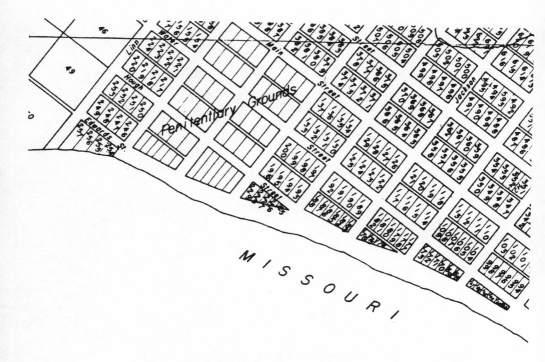

Map
of the
City of Jefferson

1849

LOT NUMBER

92 - 93	GOVERNOR'S RESIDENCE
94	RISING SUN INN (PRESENT SITE OF UNION ELECTRIC)
110	FIRST BAPTIST CHURCH (NOVEMBER 1888 - PRESENT)
326	WHITE HOUSE - BIRTHPLACE OF R. E. YOUNG
327	JOHN FRAZIER'S SCHOOL
LL 332	PRESBYTERIAN CHURCH
335	RESIDENCE OF LEVI GUNSALLUS
338	PAULSEL HOUSE (PRESENT SITE OF CENTRAL BANK)

REFERENCES ARE TO SITES DURING THE 1840S AND 1850S EXCEPT WHERE NOTED

LOT NUMBER

UH 339	EPISCOPAL CHURCH (PRESENT SITE OF PARKING GARAGE)
LL 341-LR 342	METHODIST CHURCH
LH 351	COURTHOUSE
379	WARDEN'S HOUSE (CIRCA 1888 - PRESENTLY HAWKINS' LAW)
471	THALHEIMER'S STORE (PRESENT SITE OF EXCHANGE BANK)
476	YOUNG GROCERY COMPANY (CIRCA 1900)
606	JAIL
720	BAPTIST CHRUCH

LL = LOWER LEFT   LR = LOWER RIGHT   LH = LOWER HALF   UH = UPPER HALF

APPENDIX B

~

SOLDIERS OF THE
MEXICAN WAR
MENTIONED BY DR. YOUNG*

Thaddeus Boone	Charles B. Maus	John B. Walters
William A. Curry**	Fountain McKenzie	Richard A. Wells
William Ferguson	Mosby Monroe Parsons	Benjamin W. Winston
Calvin Gunn, Jr.	Henry Paulsel	George B. Winston
William H. Lusk	Sterling Price	

       The Cole County Dragoons, which became Company F, First Missouri Mounted Volunteers, helped capture a cannon made from church bells at the battle of Chihuahua.[1] Other such cannon were captured by Doniphan's regiment at Sacramento. These cannons became war trophies and the property of the State of Missouri. One of these cannons became known as "Old Sacramento" and was notorious for its distinctive sound when fired. "Old Sacramento" saw service with the Missouri State Guard at Carthage, Oak Hills (Wilson's Creek), Lexington, and Elkhorn Tavern (Pea Ridge).[2]

* *History of Cole, Moniteau, Morgan, Benton, Miller, Maries and Osage Counties, Missouri* served as source for names. Other names can be verified with the resources of the Missouri State Archives and State Historical Society.
** William Elsey Connelley. *Doniphan's Expedition and the Conquest of New Mexico and California.* Topeka, KS: William Elsey Connelley, 1907.
[1] *History of Cole, Moniteau, Morgan, Benton, Miller, Maries and Osage Counties, Missouri.* Chicago: The Goodspeed Publishing Co., 1889.
[2] Jay Monaghan. *Civil War on the Western Border, 1854-1865.* Lincoln: University of Nebraska Press, Second cloth printing, 1992.

Appendix C

~

Soldiers of the
War Between the States
As Mentioned by Dr. Young[*]

Missouri State Guard and Confederate

"Uncle" Jake
Alfred Basye
John Basye[**]
Bill Boldridge
Lon Boyle
Amos F. Cake
James Rockne Champion
Alexander M. Davison[***]
William A. Davison[***]
Calom E. Dawson
Alexander Pope Dorris
Thomas Dorris
Henry Duncan
Jack Duncan
James T. Edwards

William Edwards
Ashley Ewing[**]
James S. Fagan
Richard Gaines
Henry Guibor
S. Hagan
Thomas C. Hindman
Theophilus Holmes
Warwick Hough[****]
John Inglish[**]
Joseph Kelly
Alexander A. Lesueur
John S. Marmaduke
Tennessee Mathews, Jr.[**]
Robert A. McCulloch

Eli Bass McHenry
Dandridge McRae
Mosby Monroe Parsons
Lebbeus Pindall
Celsus Price
Sterling Price
George Rootes
John B. Ruthven
Austin Standish
Jacob Straus
Smith Thomas
Charles B. Tilden
Lucius Marsh Walker
John Waller
Jim Woods

Union

Frank Blair, Jr.[**]
Frederick Buehrle[**]
Addison Elston[***]
Austin A. King, Jr.[**]

Edward L. King[**]
William H. Lusk[**]
Nathaniel Lyon
Charles B. Maus[**]

Phillip Thomas Miller
Thomas Lawson Price
Franz Sigel

---

[*] This list may not be inclusive. Other names can be verified with the resources of the Missouri State Archives and State Historical Society.

[**] *History of Cole, Moniteau, Miller, Maries and Osage Counties, Missouri.* Chicago: The Goodspeed Publishing Co., 1889.

[***] Joseph S. Summers, Jr., M. D. *Medical Milestones in Cole County, Missouri: A History of the Cole County Medical Society.* Jefferson City, MO: Summers Publishing, 1988. p. 42.

[****] *Index to Enrollment Cards - Civil War - Confederate.* Missouri State Archives.

Appendix D

~

Clark Township Southern Guards
Company B, First Cavalry Regiment
Sixth Division, Missouri State Guard

Captain - Fountain M. McKenzie

1st Lt. B. S. Bond	2nd Sgt. C. L. Musick	1st Cpl. R. W. Greenup
2nd Lt. Nelson Martin	3rd Sgt. A. Dover	2nd Cpl. John Dunkin
3rd Lt. Jacob Hale	4th Sgt. Joseph Johnston	3rd Cpl. John Musick
1st Sgt. J. H. Bond	5th Sgt. B. F. Clark	4th Cpl. J. F. Hale

Privates

E. G. Ballinger	Ed Green	M. B. Russell
M. M. Basinger	J. C. Greenup	W. B. Russell
M. Bass	Samuel Greenup	A. C. Simpson
C. Bass	J. T. Grimestaff	E. V. Simpson
George Berry	Preston Hale	G. V. Simpson
John Berry	J. J. Hillard (Lillard?)	J. A. Simpson
T. D. Bliss	S. L. Hubbard	J. E. Simpson
G. W. Boise	James C. Jackson	John Scott
J. R. Bond	Alfred Lee	R. Scott
W. C. Bond	J. Martin	S. L. Scott
John Bowers	J. B. McKenzie	J. Shephard
B. W. Boggs	Allige Miller	John Smith
E. Carson	Milton Moore	E. ?. Strong
H. Clark	Thos. Moran	M. E. Strong
M. D. Clark	E. Newton	J. J. Sullin
R. Crisp	S. Perkins	C. Summerhisem
L. P. Crabtree	G. W. Pervis	T. ?. Trustly
John Dunlap	James R?vis	J. Van Hooser
J. H. Davis	John Reed	J. Vaughn
E. Dixson	R. S. Rob	Allen Williams
John Dover	Willis Roberts	W. T. Wilson
Henry Duncan	W. D. Row	W. Workman
W. M. Dunklin	H. C. Russell	W. Workover

MUSTER ROLL OF 10 MAY 1861, located at the State Historical Society, transcribed by Darrell L. Maples, Adjutant - Missouri Division and Gen. M. M. Parsons Camp No. 718, Sons of Confederate Veterans. Names are spelled as they are on original document.

BIBLIOGRAPHY
Dr. Young and His Family

1. *The Grave Marker of W. C. Young and Ann F. Young.* Woodland Cemetery. Jefferson City, Missouri.
2. *History of Cole, Moniteau, Morgan, Benton, Miller, Maries and Osage Counties, Missouri.* Chicago: The Goodspeed Publishing Co., 1889. p. 903.
3. Ibid.
4. Marian M. Ohman. *Encyclopedia of Missouri Courthouses.* Columbia, MO: University of Missouri - Columbia Extension Division, 1981.
5. Ibid.
6. Ibid.
7. *History of Cole, Moniteau, Morgan, Benton, Miller, Maries and Osage Counties, Missouri.* Chicago: The Goodspeed Publishing Co., 1889. p. 368.
8. Ibid. p. 903.
9. *Missouri State Tribune* (Jefferson City, MO), December 29, 1900.
10. *Missouri State Tribune* (Jefferson City, MO), April 20, 1901.
11. *Register of Civil Proceedings*, Vol. B 10 Mar 1852 - 31 Oct 1860. p. 182, August 7, 1856. Missouri State Archives.
12. Ibid. p. 184, August 11, 1856.
13. *Register of State, National, and County Officers*, Vol. 1, p. 173, August 26, 1856. Missouri State Archives.
14. *Register of Civil Proceedings*, Vol. B 10 Mar 1852 - 31 Oct 1860. p. 260, December 30, 1856. Missouri State Archives.
15. Ibid. p. 291, August 5, 1857.
16. *Register of State, National, and County Officers*, Vol. 1, December 10, 1862. Missouri State Archives; *History of Cole, Moniteau, Morgan, Benton, Miller, Maries and Osage Counties, Missouri.* Chicago: The Goodspeed Publishing Co., 1889. p. 233.
17. *Register of Civil Proceedings*, Vol. F 13 Jun 1874 - 31 Dec 1878. p. 40, November 7, 1874. Missouri State Archives.
18. J. W. Johnston ed. *The Illustrated Sketch Book and Directory of Jefferson City and Cole County.* Jefferson City, MO: Missouri Illustrated Sketch Book Co., 1900. p. 241.
19. Joseph S. Summers. *One Hundred Fifty Years of Service A History of Jefferson Lodge #43 A.F. & A.M.* Jefferson City, MO: Jefferson Lodge #43 A.F. & A.M., 1991.
20. *The Grave Marker of W. C. Young and Ann F. Young.* Woodland Cemetery. Jefferson City, Missouri.
21. *The Daily Tribune* (Jefferson City, MO), December 25, 1883; "Half A Century," *The State Journal* (Jefferson City, MO), December 21, 1883.
22. *History of Cole, Moniteau, Morgan, Benton, Miller, Maries and Osage Counties Missouri.* Chicago: The Goodspeed Publishing Co., 1889. p. 301.
23. *The Grave Marker of W. C. Young and Ann F. Young.* Woodland Cemetery. Jefferson City, Missouri.

24. *The Young-Murphy Family Archives.* In possession of Jimmie Eckenberger, William "Billy" Murphy, and Edward L. Ziehmer.
25. *Jefferson Examiner* (Jefferson City, MO), October 13, 1855.
26. *The Young-Murphy Family Archives.*
27. Ibid.
28. Ibid.
29. Walter Lowrie ed. *Early Settlers of Missouri As Taken From Land Claims in the Missouri Territory.* Reprint. Easley, SC: Southern Historical Press, Inc, 1986. p.425.
30. Floyd Calvin Shoemaker, LL.D. *Missouri and Missourians.* Chicago: The Lewis Publishing Company, 1943. p. 97, 280.
31. Howard L. Conrad ed. *Encyclopedia of the History of Missouri*, Vol. I. St. Louis: The Southern History Company, 1901. p. 170-172.
32. Floyd Calvin Shoemaker, LL.D. *Missouri and Missourians.* Chicago: The Lewis Publishing Company, 1943. p. 279-280, 329, 523.
33. *The Young-Murphy Family Archives.*
34. Ibid.
35. Ibid.
36. Ibid.
37. *Register of State, National, and County Officers*, Vol. 2, December 17, 1900; November 20, 1902. Missouri State Archives.
38. *The Young-Murphy Family Archives.*
39. Ibid.
40. *History of Cole, Moniteau, Morgan, Benton, Miller, Maries and Osage Counties Missouri.* Chicago: The Goodspeed Publishing Co., 1889. p. 874.
41. *The Young-Murphy Family Archives.*
42. "Fred Murphy Dies of Heart Failure," *Jefferson City Post Tribune*, February 25, 1941.
43. *The Young-Murphy Family Archives.*
44. "Death of Robert E. [Lee] Murphy," *The State Journal* (Jefferson City, MO), August 17, 1883.
45. *The Young-Murphy Family Archives.*
46. Ibid.
47. Ibid.
48. Ibid.
49. Ibid.
50. Ibid. Undated Newspaper Clipping.
51. *The Young Family Archives.*
52. Ibid.
53. Mrs. Ross R. Geary. *Cemetery Record of Woodland and Old City Cemetery.* Jefferson City, MO: Jane Randolph Jefferson Chapter, NSDAR, 1976. p. 66.
54. *The Young-Murphy Family Archives.*
55. Ibid.
56. Ibid.
57. Ibid.

58. Ibid.
59. Mrs. Ross R. Geary. *Cemetery Record of Woodland and Old City Cemetery.* Jefferson City, MO: Jane Randolph Jefferson Chapter, NSDAR, 1976. p. 66.
60. *History of Cole, Moniteau, Morgan, Benton, Miller, Maries and Osage Counties, Missouri.* Chicago: The Goodspeed Publishing Co., 1889. p. 904.
61. *The Grave Marker of Ann J. Young and Ann G. Murphy.* Woodland Cemetery. Jefferson City, Missouri.
62. *History of Cole, Moniteau, Morgan, Benton, Miller, Maries and Osage Counties, Missouri.* Chicago: The Goodspeed Publishing Co., 1889. p. 903.
63. *Confederate Military History, Extended Edition,* Volume 9. Wilmington, NC: Broadfoot Publishing Company, 1988. p. 444-445.
64. *Missouri State Tribune* (Jefferson City, MO), March 30, 1901.
65. *Confederate Military History, Extended Edition,* Volume 9. Wilmington, NC: Broadfoot Publishing Company, 1988. p. 444-445.
66. *History of Cole, Moniteau, Morgan, Benton, Miller, Maries and Osage Counties, Missouri.* Chicago: The Goodspeed Publishing Co., 1889. p. 224.
67. Ibid. p. 283.
68. Ibid. p. 283.
69. Ibid. p. 283.
70. Phil Gottschalk. *In Deadly Earnest: The Missouri Brigade.* Columbia, MO: Missouri River Press, 1991. p. 13.
71. *History of Cole, Moniteau, Morgan, Benton, Miller, Maries and Osage Counties Missouri.* Chicago: The Goodspeed Publishing Co., 1889. p. 283.
72. *Confederate Military History, Extended Edition,* Volume 9. Wilmington, NC: Broadfoot Publishing Company, 1988. p. 444-445; Daleen, Keith et al. *Sterling Price's Lieutenants.* Shawnee Mission, KS: Two Trails Publishing, 1995. p. 175.
73. *Daily Missouri Republican* (St. Louis), May 14, 1861.
74. Ibid.
75. Ibid.
76. *Confederate Military History, Extended Edition,* Volume 9. Wilmington, NC: Broadfoot Publishing Company, 1988. p. 444-445.
77. *The War of the Rebellion: A Compilation of the Official Records of the Union and Confederate Armies,* Series 1, Vol. 53. Washington: Government Printing Office, 1898. p. 434.
78. *Confederate Military History, Extended Edition,* Volume 9. Wilmington, NC: Broadfoot Publishing Company, 1988. p. 69.
79. Ibid.
80. "Missouri Turned Over to the Rebel Confederacy," *The Missouri Statesman* (Columbia, MO), December 1, 1861; Devereaux D. Cannon, Jr. *The Flags of The Confederacy: An Illustrated History.* Memphis: St. Lukes Press and Broadfoot Publishing, 1988. p. 13.; Daleen, Keith et al. *Sterling Price's Lieutenants.* Shawnee Mission, KS: Two Trails Publishing, 1995. p. 175.
81. *Confederate Military History, Extended Edition,* Volume9. Wilmington, NC: Broadfoot Publishing Company, 1988. p. 444-445.
82. Ibid.

83. *Record of Missouri Confederate Veterans Compiled for The United Daughters of the Confederacy, Missouri Division.* Missouri State Archives.
84. *Confederate Military History, Extended Edition,* Volume9. Wilmington, NC: Broadfoot Publishing Company, 1988. p. 444-445.
85. Ibid.
86. Ibid.
87. *Compiled Service Records of Confederate Soldiers from Missouri; Third Field Battery.* State Historical Society.
88. *Jefferson City Daily Tribune,* July 1, 1887
89. Ibid.
90. *Confederate Military History, Extended Edition,* Volume9. Wilmington, NC: Broadfoot Publishing Company, 1988. p. 444-445.
91. Joseph S. Summers, Jr., M. D. *Medical Milestones in Cole County, Missouri: A History of the Cole County Medical Society.* Jefferson City, MO: Summers Publishing, 1988. p. 42.
92. *Register of Civil Proceedings,* Vol. E 10 Oct 1868 - 13 Jun 1874. January 21, 1873. Missouri State Archives.
93. Ibid. May 11, 1874.
94. Joseph S. Summers, Jr., M. D. *Medical Milestones in Cole County, Missouri: A History of the Cole County Medical Society.* Jefferson City, MO: Summers Publishing, 1988. p. 42.
95. *The People's Tribune* (Jefferson City, MO), April 8, 1874.
96. *History of Cole, Moniteau, Morgan, Benton, Miller, Maries and Osage Counties, Missouri.* Chicago: The Goodspeed Publishing Co., 1889. p. 247.
97. Michael K. McGrath, Secretary of State. *State Almanac and Official Directory of Missouri, for 1878.* St. Louis: John J. Daly & Co., 1878; Michael K. McGrath, Secretary of State. *Official Directory of Missouri, for 1881.* St. Louis: John J. Daly & Co., 1881; Michael K. McGrath, Secretary of State. *Official Directory of Missouri, for 1883.* St. Louis: John J. Daly & Co., 1883; Michael K. McGrath, Secretary of State. *Official Directory of Missouri, for 1885.* St. Louis: John J. Daly & Co., 1885.
98. *Journal of Proceedings, Board of Aldermen,* Vol. 3, 2 May 1872 to 12 Oct 1880. Missouri River Regional Library, Jefferson City, Missouri.
99. *History of Cole, Moniteau, Morgan, Benton, Miller, Maries and Osage Counties, Missouri.* Chicago: The Goodspeed Publishing Co., 1889. p. 307.
100. *Columbia Statesman* (Columbia, MO), February 13, 1889.
101. *Register of Civil Proceedings,* Vol. H, 2 Oct 1882 - 31 Aug 1885. January 28, 1885. Missouri State Archives.
102. *Register of Civil Proceedings,* Vol. I, 1 Sep 1885 - 29 Oct 1888. January 18, 1887. Missouri State Archives..
103. Ibid. April 15, 1886.
104. Ibid. November 4, 1887; *The Daily Mail* (Nevada, MO), June 28, 1887.
105. *History of Cole, Moniteau, Morgan, Benton, Miller, Maries and Osage Counties, Missouri.* Chicago: The Goodspeed Publishing Co., 1889. p. 874.
106. *The Missouri State Tribune* (Jefferson City), January 12, 1904.

107. *Confederate Military History, Extended Edition*, Volume9. Wilmington, NC: Broadfoot Publishing Company, 1988. p. 444-445.
108. J. W. Johnston ed. *The Illustrated Sketch Book and Directory of Jefferson City and Cole County.* Jefferson City, MO: Missouri Illustrated Sketch Book Co., 1900. p. 241.
109. Alexander A. Lesueur, Secretary of State. *Official Manual of the State of Missouri for the Years 1899-1900.* Jefferson City, MO: Tribune Printing Company, 1899.
110. *Register of Civil Proceedings*, Vol. K, 2 Jan 1893 - 31 Oct 1897. April 15, 1897. Missouri State Archives.
111. *Register of Civil Proceedings*, Vol. L, 1 Nov 1897 - 29 Jun 1901. January 31, Missouri State Archives.
112. J. W. Johnston ed. *The Illustrated Sketch Book and Directory of Jefferson City and Cole County.* Jefferson City, MO: Missouri Illustrated Sketch Book Co., 1900. p. 45-47.
113. Ibid.
114. Ibid.
115. Joseph S. Summers, Jr., M. D. *Medical Milestones in Cole County, Missouri: A History of the Cole County Medical Society.* Jefferson City, MO: Summers Publishing, 1988. p. 42.
116. Ibid.
117. "One of City's Best Known Women is Dead At Age of 86," *Jefferson City Tribune*, October 9, 1926.
118. *The People's Tribune* (Jefferson City, MO), May 21, 1873.
119. *The Young-Murphy Family Archives.*
120. "One of City's Best Known Women is Dead At Age of 86," *Jefferson City Tribune*, October 9, 1926.
121. *Record of Missouri Confederate Veterans Compiled for The United Daughters of the Confederacy, Missouri Division.* Missouri States Archives.
122. J. W. Johnston ed. *The Illustrated Sketch Book and Directory of Jefferson City and Cole County.* Jefferson City, MO: Missouri Illustrated Sketch Book Co., 1900. p. 161, 169.
123. "Dr. Young is Dead," *The Democrat Tribune* (Jefferson City, MO), September 27, 1915.
124. *Record of Missouri Confederate Veterans Compiled for The United Daughters of the Confederacy, Missouri Division.* Missouri State Archives.
125. J. W. Johnston ed. *The Illustrated Sketch Book and Directory of Jefferson City and Cole County.* Jefferson City, MO: Missouri Illustrated Sketch Book Co., 1900. p. 165
126. "Young-Ruwart. Popular Young People Unite in Marriage," *Missouri State Tribune* (Jefferson City, MO), October 23, 1901.
127. *Record of Missouri Confederate Veterans Compiled for The United Daughters of the Confederacy, Missouri Division.* Missouri State Archives; "One of City's Best Known Women is Dead At Age of 86," *Jefferson City Tribune*, October 9, 1926.
128. "The Death of Dr. Young," *Missouri State Tribune*, January 9, 1904.

SOURCES OF ILLUSTRATIONS

PAGE

2   **1859 JEFFERSON CITY,** Eduard Robyn, View of Jefferson City, 1859. Photograph courtesy of Missouri State Archives, Dr. Joseph Summers Collection.

2   **THE YOUNG FAMILY TREE,** Edward L. Ziehmer.

4   **WILLIAM CAMPBELL YOUNG,** Young-Murphy Family Archives, in possession of Jimmie Eckenberger, William "Billy" Murphy, and Ed Ziehmer.

14   **THE YOUNG FAMILY MONUMENTS,** Photograph by Mark S. Schreiber.

15   **DR. ROBERT EMMET YOUNG,** Young-Murphy Family Archives.

16   **THE YOUNG RESIDENCE ON MAIN STREET,** Young-Murphy Family Archives.

17   **THE YOUNG RESIDENCE TODAY,** Photograph by Mark S. Schreiber.

18   **WILLIAM CAMPBELL YOUNG, II,** Young-Murphy Family Archives.

19   **JAMES MCKENNA YOUNG,** Young-Murphy Family Archives.

20   **DR. YOUNG IN HIS OFFICE,** Young-Murphy Family Archives.

22   **GENERAL LYON'S CHARGE AT WILSON'S CREEK,** F. O. C. Darley. Courtesy of Mark S. Schreiber

27   **JOHN SAPPINGTON MARMADUKE,** Courtesy of State Historical Society, Columbia, Missouri.

37   **MOSBY MONROE PARSONS,** Young-Murphy Family Archives.

43   **THE OLD COURTHOUSE,** Eduard Robyn, View of Jefferson City, 1859. From original, courtesy of Mark S. Schreiber.

61   **JEFFERSON INQUIRER PRINTING OFFICE,** Eduard Robyn, View of Jefferson City, 1859. From original, courtesy of Mark S. Schreiber.

65   **THE OLD EXECUTIVE OFFICE AND MANSION,** Eduard Robyn, View of Jefferson City, 1859. Courtesy of Missouri State Archives, Dr. Joseph Summers Collection.

PAGE

85   THE STATE CAPITOL OF 1840, Eduard Robyn, View of Jefferson City, 1859.
     From original, courtesy of Mark S. Schreiber.

87   THE FERGUSON HOUSE, Eduard Robyn, View of Jefferson City, 1859. From
     original, courtesy of Mark S. Schreiber.

89   THOMAS LAWSON PRICE, Thomas Lawson Price's monument in Riverview
     Cemetery, photograph by Mark S. Schreiber.

91   PRICE MANSION, J. W. Johnston ed. *The Illustrated Sketch Book and
     Directory of Jefferson City and Cole County.* Jefferson City, MO: Missouri
     Illustrated Sketch Book Co., 1900. p. 303. Courtesy of Missouri State
     Archives, Dr. Joseph Summers Collection.

93   BURR HARRISON MCCARTY, J. W. Johnston ed. *The Illustrated Sketch Book
     and Directory of Jefferson City and Cole County.* Jefferson City, MO:
     Missouri Illustrated Sketch Book Co., 1900. p. 299.

97   WILLIAM H. LUSK, J. W. Johnston ed. *The Illustrated Sketch Book and
     Directory of Jefferson City and Cole County.* Jefferson City, MO: Missouri
     Illustrated Sketch Book Co., 1900. p. 280.

109 NEWMAN'S CITY HOTEL, Eduard Robyn, View of Jefferson City, 1859. From
     original, courtesy of Mark S. Schreiber.

113 CONFEDERATE SOLDIERS, Artist Unkown. Collection of Edward L. Ziehmer.

134 EDWARD LIVINGSTON EDWARDS, J. W. Johnston ed. *The Illustrated Sketch
     Book and Directory of Jefferson City and Cole County.* Jefferson City, MO:
     Missouri Illustrated Sketch Book Co., 1900. p. 378.

144 THOMAS MILLER WINSTON, J. W. Johnston ed. *The Illustrated Sketch Book
     and Directory of Jefferson City and Cole County.* Jefferson City, MO:
     Missouri Illustrated Sketch Book Co., 1900. p. 399.

151 PHILLIP THOMAS MILLER, J. W. Johnston ed. *The Illustrated Sketch Book
     and Directory of Jefferson City and Cole County.* Jefferson City, MO:
     Missouri Illustrated Sketch Book Co., 1900. p. 345.

153 CLONEY, CRAWFORD & CO., Eduard Robyn, View of Jefferson City, 1859.
     From original, courtesy of Mark S. Schreiber.

162 SIGNATURE OF DR. YOUNG, Young-Murphy Family Archives.

178 PRIVATE ROBERT "BOB" E. YOUNG, Young-Murphy Family Archives.

INDEX

?, "Uncle Jake"   105
Abbott   55
Ainsworth, Bill   69
Ainsworth, Bob   69,145
Ainsworth, Mrs.   69
Ainsworth, Robert   145
Ainsworth, William   145
Alton, Illinois   159
Anderson, Frank   40,82
Anderson, Tham.   82
Anderson, William   6
Arkadelphia, Ark.   105
Arrow Rock, Missouri   165
Athens, Ga.   181
Atlanta, Ga.   181
Bancroft   see Barcroft
Baptist Church   59,104
Barcroft   119
Barcroft house   62
Barcroft, Major   45
Barnes, "Uncle" Howard   74
Barrett, Dr.   165
Bartlett   75
Barton, David   6
Basey House   63,72
Basey mansion   66
Basey, Alfred;Dr.   73
        Major 146
Basey, John   65,73
Basey, Major   47,72-73
Basye   see Basey
Bauer, John   119
Bay, Mrs.   57
Bay, Widow   57
Bedot, Widow   122
Belch, Mrs. J. Ed.   13
Benton, Col. Thomas Hart
        36,70,74,87-88,90,
        96,100,141
Berry Farm   76
Berry, Dr.   123
Berry, Green   38
Berry, John   147
Berry, Mrs.   123
Binder's Park   119
Binder, Fred H.   185
Bingham, Prof.   69
Black Hawk   92,93-94
Blair, Frank P.   90,150
Blevins, Jim   40

Boggs' administration
        42,44,55
Boggs' Hill   158
Boggs, Lilburn; Governor
        36,42,44,55,158
Boggs, Henry   158
Boggs, James   158
Boggs, Mr.   158
Bohanan, Miss Bettie   100
Bohn mansion   35
Bohn, Al   35
Bohn, Sallie   35
Boldridge, Bill   116
Bolton, Cecelia   76
Bolton, Gen.   98
Bolton, Josephine   77
Bolton, Miss   90
Bolton, Ophelia   77
Bolton, Sarah Landsdown 76
Bolton, Theodosia   77
Bolton, William; Dr.   76
Boone, Thaddeus   55,96,98
Boonville, Missouri
    first battle of   28
Boston   7
Boyle, Lon   29
Breckenridge Democracy   88
Brown's Row   62
Brown, Gratz   82; Gov.   62
Brownsville, Missouri   165
Buehrle, Col.   104
Burch   55,96
Burch, Oscar G.   176
Burger, Fred   92
Burger, Henry   92
Burlingame, Hazel
        106,154-155
Burr   94
Burr, Eph   96
Busse, Dr.   165
Cache River   see Cash River
Cake, Amos F.; Capt.   116
California road   119
California, Missouri   160
Callahan, Miss Mollie   99
Callahan, Mrs.   110
Callahan, Widow   99
Callaway County 98,103,116
Camden County Courthouse 3
Camden, Arkansas   10
Carr, Squire   102

Carstarphen, George B. 176
Carthage, battle of 9,103 111
Cash river 114
Cassville, Missouri 25
Catholic Church 54
Cedar City, Missouri 102
Central Hotel 99
Centertown Cemetery 6-7
Centretown, Missouri 4,30,81
Champion, Captain James Rockne "Rock" 25,170,177
Chapman, Steve 50
Chappell 102,103,124
Chappell, John 127
Chappell, Phil. 102,127,128,151,152
Chase, Widow 98
Chicago 159
Chihuahua, battle of 39
Chillicothe, Missouri 165
Christian Church 59
Christy, Reed 62
Church, H. B., Sr. 107
City Hotel 3,59,95,99, 110,111,132
Claggett, Mr. 51
Clark Township Southern Guards 9
Clark's Row 79
Clark, B. F. 182
Clark, Dr. 176
Clark, W. A. 183
Clay, Henry 145,150
Cloney, Crawford & Co. 143,152
Cobb, Mary Ann 181
Cole County Medical Society 12, 172,176,180,183
Cole County poor farm 168-169
Coleman, Stepehen O.; Lieutenant-Colonel 25
Columbia, Missouri 8,46,62,165,166,171
Cordell residence 36
Cordell, Dick 57,77

Cordell, E. B. 57,76, 90,128
Cordell, E. B. & Co. 128
Cordell, Ed. 38
Cordell, Enos 57
Cordell, Ern 65
Cordell, Ernest 34,155
Cordell, Harry 57,77
Cordell, Henry 57,75, 77,151; Mrs. 57
Cordell, Mrs. 54,77
Cordell, Tom 57,77
Corinth, Mississippi 10
Cox, Mrs. 58
Crandall see Crandell
Crandel, Frank 155
Crandel, John 155
Crandell, Floyd 107
Crawford, T. L. 143
Crittenden, Thomas T. 152
Crockett, Samuel 165
Cumberland Presbyterian Church 4
Cummins, A. 165
Curry, J. D.
Curry, John 100
Curry, John D. 100
Curry, Mrs. 100-101
Curry, William 100,111; Dr. 100,111-112
Daber, Al 96
Dagmar, Queen 182
Dallmeyer Building 13
Dallmeyer, Mr. Rudolph 129
Davis, President Jefferson 181
Davis, Winnie see Winnie Davis Chapter, UDC
Davison 125,141
Davison, Alex. M.; Dr. 50,69,108,111
Davison, William; Dr. 108-109
Dawson, Calom E. 114-115
Dean, Mary 142
Dean, Widow 142
Dean, William 142
Declaration of Independence 60

Deepwater, Missouri 165
Dellinger see Dillinger
Dellinger family 4,13
Dellinger, Catherine 4,13
Dellinger, Henry 4,13
Delmonico 78
Dewey, Charles E. 176
Dillinger, Grandmother
        140
Dillinger, Miss Ellen 99
Dixon, Ann 135,136
Dixon, Frank M. 127
Dixon, "Uncle Hal" 95
Dixon, Warren 135,136
Doniphan's regiment
        39,111
Doniphan, Alexander W.
        39
Dorris, Alexander Pope
        55,96,127;
        Dr. 100,101-103,
        104,127,145;
        Mrs. 102-103
Dorris, McDaniel
        107,138
Dorris, Thomas 102,103
Dunscomb, Ed.; Mrs. 159
Dunscomb, Elizabeth 55
Dunscomb, Wm. E.
        127-128,151
Duncan, Henry 139
Duncan, Jack 139
Duncan, John 138-139
Dunlap, A. W.; Mrs. 81
Dunica, James; Col. 83-84
Dunnica see Dunica
Edwards 40,141
Edwards, Alice 127
Edwards, Ann 137
Edwards, Edward L.; Judge
        41,67,70,120,132-137
Edwards, Ernest 127
Edwards, Gen. 40
Edwards, J. H.; Dr. 124-127
Edwards, J. R. 128;
        Mrs. 159
Edwards, James T.
        24-25
Edwards, John 127
Edwards, John C.; Governor
        65,67,70,132,136

Edwards, John W. 136
Edwards, Joseph R. 136
Edwards, Margaret 127
Edwards, Sallie 136
Edwards, Thomas 127
Edwards, Walter 127
Edwards, William 136
Elkhorn Tavern, battle of
        10 see also Pea Ridge
Elston, Addison; Dr. 54
Elston, Missouri 168
English, Judge John 147
Enloe, I. N.; Dr. 176,183
Episcopal church 54,62,63
Ewing's station 159
Ewing, Ashley 160
Ewing, E.; Mrs 51
Ewing, Eph 38,96
Ewing, Ephriam 160
Ewing, Gilson 160
Ewing, H. Clay 38,160;
        Judge Clay 107
Ewing, Robert 160
Ewing, Robert A.; Judge
        4,159,160
Fackler, Rev. John G. 78
Fagan, Gen. James S.
        114,115-116
Farmington, Missouri 6
Faust, Tony 78
Ferguson House 86-87
Ferguson, Mrs. 86
Ferguson, Wm. 86
Fischer, Gus 101
Fisher, W. I. 165
Fitzsimmons, Mary 96
Fletcher, Minerva Ann 6
Fort Curtis 115
Fort El-Canay 118
Fort Leavenworth 99
Fourth of July 60-61,104,
        116
Fowler 160
Fowler, Judge 184
Francis, Gov. 173
Frazer see also Frazier
Frazer, Henry 92
Frazer, John 92
Frazer, Jim 92
Frazier see also Frazer
Frazier, Mrs. 63

Friemel's Garden   145
Fulkerson   85
Gabbett, Mrs. S. E.   181
Gaines   see Gains
Gains, Col. Richard   26
Gantt, Jas. B.   178
Gantt, Judge J. B.   182
Gantt, Mrs.   182
Gardenhire   40
Gardenhire, James B.;
      Col.   100
Gasconade bridge   50,60
Gass, H. A.   185
Gesteranus, Mase   143
Gettysburg, battle of
      10,118
Geyer, Henry S.   88
Gibbler, Joseph
      168-169
Gibbler, Mrs.   168-169
Gibler   see Gibbler
Gielow, Mrs.   182
Glenn   160
Globe clothing   123
Glover's mill   140
Glover, Peter   128
Gordon   55
Gordon, Dr.   165
Gordon, John C.   50,51,
      73
Gordon, John W.; Mrs.   54
Gorham's battery   10
Grace church 66
Gray's creek   100
Greene   75
Grimshaw Bros.   119
Guibor's battery   10,23-24
Guibor, Henry   23
Guinnea, Africa   129
Guinny Joe   129-130
Guire see Geyer, Henry S.
Gunn residence   72
Gunn, Ben   96
Gunn, Cal   40,71,73
Gunn, Calvin   63,71
Gunn, Mary   62
Gunsallus   see Gunsaullis
Gunsaullis, Levi   100;
      Col.   101
Hagan, S.   114-115
Hall, Charles Edward   7

Hall, William C.   7
Handly grocery store
      75
Harper, Joe   173
Harrison Campaign
      55,74,126
Harrison, Gen.   74
Harrison, Squire Jason
      35
Harrison, William H.   55
Hart Estate   58
Hart, "Auntie Mariah"   58
Hart, Dr.   165
Hart, "Uncle Billy"   58
Hayden   40,41,42,132,133
Heim, Abe   108
Heinrichs' furniture   63
Helena, Arkansas   10,28,
      113,114,115
Helena, battle of   10,
      113-118
Helena, Montana   127
Hendy's blacksmith shop
      62
Hendy, Dr. J. F.   180
Henry County   165
Henry, Gen.   26
Henry, Jesse W.   50,185
Hereford school   66,68-70,
      71,73,82,92
Hereford, Frank   63-64,68,
      72
Hervidian Hotel   74
Hindman, Gen. Thomas C.
      113
Hobbs, Major V. M.   176
Hobo Hill   106,154-157
Hockaday   29
Hockaday, Judge John A.
      174
Holmes, Gen. Theophilus
      114,115,118
Hough, Arthur   59
Hough, Charley   59
Hough, Chas. P.   183
Hough, Dr.   176
Hough, George W.   59,60,
      110
Hough, Laura   59-60
Hough, Nathaniel   33,59,
      65,155

Hough, Warwick   40,59
Hunter   98
Hughes, Mr. 139
Inglish   see English
Inquirer 96
Isbell, Harvey W.   165
Ivy Terrace   52,54
Jackson County, Missouri 7
Jackson, Camp 8
Jackson, Camp Stonewall
        113
Jackson, Claiborne   8-9,88
Jacksonport, Arkansas 113,
        114
James, Billy   64,130
James, Widow   130
January, D. A.   25
Jefferson   141
Jefferson House   100
Jefferson City
   Land Company   100
Jefferson Lodge   128,172,
        176,180
Jefferson, Maryweather   83
Jefferson, R. L.   128
Jefferson, Robert   151
Jefferson, Robert L.   159
Jefferson, Thomas   36
Jeffersonian   63,71
Jenkin's Ferry
        battle of   10,28
Johnson's Island, Illinois
        159
Kaiser, Mrs.   59-60
Kansas City, Missouri
        111,112,127
Kansas City Real
   Estate Index   167
Kelly's infantry   23-25
Kelly, Colonel Joseph
        23-25
Kelly, William J.   42
Kennedy, D. C.   165
Kentucky Saloon   68
Kerr, Lucius   38,99
Kerr, Mrs.   110
Kerr, Wm. D.   99
Kinderhook   52
King's administration   111
King, Austin   54,155

King, Austin A.; Governor
        155
King, E. L.   54,154
King, Edward   155
King, Thomas   155
Kingsberry, Mrs.   110
Knights of the
        Golden Circle   88
Knott, J. Proctor   132
Lamb, Brother   76
Lamb, Mr.   85
Lamb, Sister   76
Lamkin, Josiah   148
Lee, Gen. Robert E.   181
Legg, S. H.   4
Leonard   58,132
Lesueur   116
Lesueur, Alexander A.   10,
        28; Captain   28,171;
        Lieutenant   114,117
Lesueur's Light Battery
        10,116,166
Lexington, battle of 9,103
Lincoln Institute   11-12
Lincoln's proclamation 143
Lincoln, Abraham   8,49,96
Linn Creek, Missouri   6
Lisle, Dan   54
Lisle, Dollie   54
Lisle, Jane   54
Lisle, Sue   54
Lisle, Widow   54
Lisletown, Missouri   161
Little Rock, Arkansas
        28,113
Locust Grove   67,97
Lohman, Missouri   7
Long, Mariah   160
Long, H. W.; Judge   138
Louisiana, 19th   105
Louisiana, Third   25
Lusk   96
Lusk, Bill   55
Lusk, James   96
Lusk, Major   151
Lusk, Martha   99
Lusk, Mary Ann   99
Lusk, William   96
Lynn, Dr.   79,101
Lynn, Duncan   33,38; Dr.
        68

Lynn, Mrs. 33
Lynn, Nat 33-34,65
Lynn, Nathaniel 33
Lyon, Gen. Nathaniel 25
Mack, Auntie Bettie 58
Madison House 29,63,74,
    75,151
Magerley, Mr. 105-106
Manchester, Mr. 35
Maries County 68
Maries Creek 48
Marmaduke's
  Administration 12,51
Marmaduke's division 114
Marmaduke, John Sappington
    11-12,26-32;
    Governor 11,13,26,
    29-32,166,173,174;
    General 28-29,
    115-116
Marmaduke Park 12,179
Mart, Miss 57
Mathews, Tennessee 84;
    Dr. 104,142
Mathews, Mr. 84
Mathews, Tenne 65
Mathews, Tenny 140
Maus, Charles 100
McCarty House 141-142
McCarty livery stable
    92,95
McCarty, Alzira 79,
    141-142
McCarty, Burr H. 92-95,
    139,141-142
McCarty, Billy 65
McCarty, Charles; Mrs. 159
McCarty, Ella 142
McClain, Peter 79
McClure, James R. 8
McClure, Carlton Moore 8
McClure, William Young 8
McClurg, Joseph W. 6
McClurg, Murphy & Co. 6
McCracken, Bob 52
McCracken, John 51-52
McCulloch, Robert A. 9,23
McCulloch's cavalry
    23,25,111,166
McHenry, Eli Bass
    34,65,84,155

McHenry, Brother 76
McHenry, George 84
McHenry, James 84
McHenry, Mr. 84
McIntyre, Gen. 58
McKenna see also McKennan
McKenna, Charlotte 13
McKennan, Charlotte 172
McKenzie's company 23
McKenzie, Fountain 9,23,
    110,111; Capt. 111
McRae's brigade 113,115
McRae, Dandridge 113
Meredith, Dangerfield 83
Melton, "Uncle" Joel 55
Memphis, Tenn. 10,84
Methodist church 52,54,
    62,78,86,142,145,
    176,180,181
Methodist parsonage 58
Metropolitan 52
Mexican War 86,111,112
Mexico, City of 112
Mexico, Old 30
Miller County 111
Miller's Creek 33
Miller's saloon 110
Miller, Bettie 79
Miller, Bill 99
Miller, Billy 38
Miller, Brother 104
Miller, Fred 104
Miller, George 77,153
Miller, George W. 136,146;
    Judge 146-148,136
Miller, Jacob 104
Miller, John 104
Miller, Louisa 77,149-150
Miller, Mrs. Wm. E. 99
Miller, P. T. 57,75,77,
    96,121,149-153,154
Miller, Pete 79
Miller, Peter 104,105
Miller, Thomas 128,150,
    152
Miller, Tom 57
Mills Inn 84
Mills, Dr. 59
Mills, Mr. 84
Mills, Thos. 84
Mills, Thom. 59

Minor, General James L.
42,44,55-56
Mississippi River 6,10,49,
114,116
Missouri Pacific 30,33,60
91,143,159,172
Missouri Penitentiary 4,
11,152,33,50,82,
110-111
Missouri River 33-35,50,
74,79,84,95
Missouri State Guard 8-10
Missouri State Medical
Association 183
Missouri State Militia 3
Missouri, 10th 115,116
Missouri, 11th 115
Missouri, 16th 115,116
Missouri, Third 10,28
Moniteau county 42,147,159
Moniteau County Courthouse
3
Munro, W. P. 165
Monroe House 97
Moore's stable 62
Moore, Harry C. 179
Moreau River 11,140,
158-159
Moreau, North 147
Moreau, South 147
Mormon War 36
Morrison, Alfred 151
Morrow, Judge 39,83
Murphy, Ann G. 6,8,13
Murphy, Edward Anderson 6
Murphy, Edward Gustavious
6-7,13
Murphy, Edward Shay 7
Murphy, F. Y. Jr. 7
Murphy, Frederick Young
6,12
Murphy, George E. 7
Murphy, Gustavious McClure
7
Murphy, Helen 7
Murphy, Hervey Ayres 7
Murphy, Kenneth 7
Murphy, Mary Catherine 6-7
Murphy, Rev. William 6
Murphy, Robert Gustavious
6

Murphy, Robert Lee 7
Murphy, Sarah Barton 6
Murphy, William Dubart 6
Murphy, William Emmet 6,7,
12
Murphy's Ford 6-7
Murphy's Settlement 6
Napton 40,41-42,58,132;
Judge 41,42
Neef residence 96
Nevada Fair Association 11
Nevada, Missouri 11,12,
165-167
New Eldorado 51
New Orleans 104
Newman, Harding 110
Newman, Maggie 110
Newman, Michael 99,110
Nickerson, Edmonda 182
O'Malley, Charley 24
Oak Hills, battle of 9
see also Wilson's Creek
Obermayer corner 83
Obermayer, Joe 111
Obermayer, Morris 111
Obermayer, Simon 111
Old City Cemetery 7,13
Ohio River 49
Osage County 111
Osage railway bridge 159
Osage River 48,98,105,
160-161
Ott's lumberyard 79
Ott, Louis 79
Owens, George 97
Owens, John 97
Owens, Sam 38,40,65,73
Owens, Sherwood 111
Parsons 40,49,141
Parsons' Brigade 103,113,
115
Parsons' Camp of United
Confederate Veterans
12-13,177-178,
181-182
Parsons, Gen. 41
Parsons, Gustavus A.;
General 36-37,39,88
141-142
Parsons, Julia 37
Parsons, July 37

Parsons, Mildred 37
Parsons, Mosby Monroe;
     Captain 39,40,49,
     86,101,111; General
     9-10,13,23,24,26,28,
     37,39-40,111,113,
     129,141,147,170,171,
     177
Parsons, Patience 37
Patillo, C. E.; Dr. 180;
     Rev. 172,176
Paulsel House 84,99,110
Paulsel, Henry 110
Pea Ridge, battle of
     10,103
     see also Elkhorn Tavern
Penninger, Brother 77
Penninger, Sister 77
Penninger, Wm. 77
Perry, John 75
Phelps County 136
Phelps, Governor John S.
     29
Philadelphia 8,12,166
Pindall's battalion 116
Pindall's sharpshooters
     115
Pindall, Lebbeus;
     Major 114
Pleasant Hill, battle of
     10
Pondrom, John C. 11
Pope 55
Porth, Dr. J. P. 84
Potomac River 49
Pratt, Mrs. 131
Pratt, W. D. 120-121,131,
     139
Presbyterian Church 54,57,
     75-79,84,150,180
Price mansion 92
Price's administration
     111
Price's army 23-25,136
Price's division 114,115
Price, Celeste 80-81,88
Price, Celsus; Capt. 117;
     Col. 81
Price, Napolean 90

Price, Sterling; General
     9,23,113,115,117;
     Governor 4
Price, Thomas 91
Price, Thomas Lawson;
     General 3,81,83-84,
     87-91,99,143
Pulliam 130,131
R., John Smith 45-48,73
Ramsey, Jonathan 160
Rader, Perry 56,58
Rector 49,129
Red River Campaign 10
Reid's Laundry 63
Rhodes, Bill 102-103
Rice 146
Richmond Hill 84
Rising Sun Inn 46,63
Robinson, Bettie 143
Robinson, Dr. J. F. 173
Robinson, Jack 143
Robinson, Lanson 158-159
Robinson, Widow 142-143
Rodgers, Capt. 35
Rodgers, Jefferson T. 84
Rogers 141
     see also Rodgers
Rogers' landing 102
Rogers, Mrs. 79
Rolla, Missouri 136
Rollins, General 46-48
Rollins, Major 62
Rootes see Roots
Roots, Bettie 79
Roots, Betty 56
Roots, George 34,56,65,
     155
Ross, Wm. 74
Ruthven, John B.; Major
     105
Ruwart, Henry 131,176
St. Charles, Missouri
     39,117,128
St. Clair County 105
St. Joseph, Missouri
     58,78,127,165
St. Louis 7,8,9,11,25,29,
     45,47,50,58,59,81,
     95,98,99,100,106,
     127,129,141,143
St. Louis road 158

Sacramento, battle of 39
Saline County 26,125,138
Sandford, Major 82-83
Schott saloon 75
Schwartzott, Adam 65
Scott 40,58,132
Scott, Judge 44,58
Secession ticket 132
Sedalia, Missouri 30,142
Seibert, James M. 128
Senate chamber 54
Shackels, Peter 131
Sharp, Mrs. 101
Sharp's House 23
Sheley, James K. 7
Sheley, Josephine 7
Shelton 55,96
Shipley's ferry 161
Sigel, General Franz 25
Sinks, M. R. 129
Smith 102
Smith, Dr. T. R. H. 166
Smith, General Jackson L.
      101
Smith, John
        see John Smith R.
          and John Smith T.
Sone, Jim 107
Sone, Sam 39,83
Spanish government 6
Spanish-American War 118
Springfield, Missouri
      23-24,165
Standish, Austin;
        Capt. 23; Col. 25
State Medical Society 172
Steele, George 40,65,
      71-72,73
Stephens'
   administration 152,172
Stephens, Lon V.; Gov. 52
Stephens, Hugh 176
Stewart, B. F. 167
Stewart, Charly 110-111
Stewart, Robert M.;
        Governor 57,82
Stone, Gov. 173
Straub, Wendell 58
Straus Saddle and
   Harness Company 106
Straus, Jacob 106
Straus, Jake 155

T., John Smith 73
        see John Smith R.
Tarlton 102,103
Taylor's administration 48
Taylor, President Zachary
      48
Thalheimer's store
      83,108,111
Thespian Society 39,40
Thomas, Smith 116
Thompkins, Judge 119
Thompson, C. A.;
        Mrs. Dr. 63
Thompson, Maria 63
Thorpe, Dr. 176
Thorpe, Dr. J. L. 95
Tilden, Charles B.;
        Capt. 114
Todd 40; Judge 41,42,44
Towles, Thomas O. 178
Trans-Mississippi
   Department, C.S.A.
      10,114
True, Geo. P. 170
Tucker, J. J. 165
Uncapher see Uncopher
Uncopher, John 131-132
United Confederate
   Veterans
        see Parsons' Camp of
          Confederate Veterans
United Daughters of the
   Confederacy 181-182
Upper Jefferson 100
Vernon county, Mo. 105,167
Vicksburg, Mississippi
      10,118
Virginia Hotel 99
Virginia, Army of Northern
      10
Walker corner 55
Walker, General Lucius
   Marsh 28
Walker, Geo. 54
Walker, Miss Rachel 54
Waller, John 117
Walters, John B. 84-85
Waltons 161
Wardsville, Missouri
      135,136
Ware's Creek 33,34,82,84,
      86

Ware, Clem 140
Warrensburg, Missouri 182
Warth, Dr. E. J. 165
Washington's Birthday 104
Washington, D. C. 129
Watson, Christy 38
Weatherby, D. C. 96
Wegman, Henry 52-53
Weiser & Artz 90,111
Wells 40
Wells, Amanda 80-81
Wells, Billy 38,71,73
Wells, Josephine 49
Wells, Judge 71
Wells, Mary 49,129
Wells, R. A. 48; Judge
    45-50,129
Wells, Richard 111-112;
    Dr. 112
Wells, William 49,129
White River 113,114
White, George T. 119-120
Wilburn, Mrs. 50
Wilburn, Thomas 51
Wilson Creek 25
Wilson's Creek
    9,23-25,103,170,177
Winnie Davis Chapter
    181-182
    see also
       United Daughters
       of the Confederacy
Winston 149
Winston, Benjamin 146
Winston, Benjamin W. 55,96
Winston, "Darb" 146
Winston, George 146
Winston, George Bickerton
    96; Dr. 112
Winston, Mrs. Dr. 59
Winston, Thomas 146
Winston, Thos. 145-146
Woodland Cemetery 6,8,13
Woods, Jim 118
Woodson, Gov. 166,167
Woodson, Silas 172
Wright County Courthouse 3
Yantis, Van Court 30
Yost, Mr. 142
Young 141,160
Young Grocery Company
    13,119

Young, Ann 13,70,77
Young, Ann Friend 4-8,13;
    "*my mother*" 50,57,
    59,71,99,100-101,
    108,140
Young, Ann J. 6,8
Young, Anna 59,60
Young, Catherine 184
Young, Charlotte
    see also
       Catherine Young
Young, James 173
Young, James M. 184
Young, James Mckenna 13
    see also
    James McKennan Young
Young, James McKennan
    172
Young, Josephine C. 6-8,
    37,77,79
Young, Mary Catherine 6-
    7,37,70,77
Young, Moses 3
Young, Robert Emmet 3,6,
    8-13,77,170; Dr. 3,
    10-13,30,56,165,166,
    167,170,171,172,173,
    174,175,176,177,179,
    180,182,183,184,185;
    Sir Knight 185
Young, William Campbell
    3-6,13,77; Colonel
    3-4; Dr. 172,173,
    184; Judge 3-8,170;
    "*my father*" 24,34,
    40,41,42-44,48,49,
    50,51,52,64,67,69,
    70,71,76,88,90,95,
    105,109,110,119,125,
    132,135,137,139,140,
    141,142,146,152,154,
    158,160
Yows, Ollie 7